PRINTING OCCUPATIONAL EMPLOYMENT, HIGH-WAGE JOBS, & INDUSTRY SOURCES OF GROWTH – 2001 TO 2005

Maryellen R. Kelley, Ph.D.

Foreword by Patricia Sorce, Ph.D.

R·I·T **Printing Industry Center**
An Alfred P. Sloan Foundation Center

Printing Industry Center
Rochester Institute of Technology
College of Imaging Arts and Sciences
55 Lomb Memorial Drive
Rochester, NY 14623
http://print.rit.edu

A Research Publication of the Printing Industry Center at RIT

Printed in the United States by Lulu.com
ISBN: 978-0-6151-9979-5

ABOUT THE AUTHOR

Maryellen R. Kelley is the President of Pamet Hill Associates, a consulting group that specializes in economic analyses of innovation and government policy, including assessments of the impacts of technological change on industry and occupations. Dr. Kelley has over 15 years of experience in advising industry and government agencies. She holds a Ph.D. in Management from the Massachusetts Institute of Technology, was awarded a Masters degree from Harvard University's Graduate School of Design, and received a B.A. from Brandeis University.

From 1997 to 2000, Dr. Kelley served as the Senior Economist in the Economic Assessment Office of the Advanced Technology Program at the National Institute of Standards and Technology, where she was responsible for developing an inter-disciplinary program of research on the innovation process and business strategies for commercializing new technologies. She has also held faculty positions at Carnegie Mellon University, the Massachusetts Institute of Technology, and the University of Massachusetts.

Dr. Kelley has authored more than 50 publications. Her papers have appeared in such journals as *Defense & Peace Economics, Economics of Innovation and New Technology, Economic Development Quarterly, Economic Geography, Industrial Relations, International Journal of Technology Management, Management Science, Research Policy, Science* and *Technology Review*.

For additional information, contact:

Maryellen Kelley
Pamet Hill Associates
P.O. Box 636
Truro, MA 02666
Phone: (508) 349-7141
E-mail: maryellen.kelley@hughes.net

TABLE OF CONTENTS

LIST OF TABLES

The Printing Industry Center is pleased to sponsor this research conducted by Dr. Maryellen Kelley on the occupational changes in the U.S. printing industries from 2001 to 2005. In a thorough analysis of the data reported by the U.S. Bureau of Labor Statistics, she tracks the growth and decline of occupations in three areas specific to the printing industry: design and prepress, print production, and post-press. However, this study also includes printing employment in industries where print production is not a main NAICS classification, which is a new contribution to the study of printing employment. Dr. Kelley also reviews the industries with more high-wage jobs in these specific occupations.

The years 2000 to 2002 were not friendly to the printing industry and many other industries as the U.S. economy struggled to move through a recession. Dr. Kelley notes that employment in the printing industry reached its peak in 1998, but that the industry as a whole did not experience substantial job losses until 2001. Overall, the printing industry lost 31,694 jobs between 2000 and 2001, with an additional loss of 58,900 jobs from 2001 to 2002.

In this sea of unpleasant news for the printing industry, the renewal of job creation can become lost. Though net employment was down by nearly 23,000 in this five-year period, 71,697 new jobs were added within the core printing occupations. Additionally, this job creation extended across a wide range of industries. As an example, the **Prof & Biz** industry group (defined by Dr. Kelley as including advertising, law, accounting, architecture and engineering, software design, computer programming and data processing services), added 28,500 jobs in this time period. This was an increase of nearly 3 times as many jobs—a ratio of 2.8:1—as the second-largest increase by the printing industry (as it is defined by NAICS codes).

As the baby-boomers move towards retirement, every industry is scrambling to find the next generation of employees to move their businesses forward. If an industry is seen as being in decline, it then has a huge public relations problem to overcome when attracting new employees. We hope that this report will provide the facts that will help printing businesses to put a positive light on future careers in printing.

Patricia Sorce, Ph.D.
Administrative Chair, School of Print Media
Co-Director, Printing Industry Center
Rochester Institute of Technology

This report focuses on employment in six occupations. The major tasks specific to these occupations are uniquely identified with the printing production process. Taken together, the selected occupations encompass all three stages of the process in the manufacture of a print product – Design/Prepress, Print Production, and Postpress. The analysis addresses the following questions:

> ➤ How many workers were employed in such printing occupations in 2001 and 2005?

> ➤ Which occupations employed the most workers in each year?

> ➤ How much has employment decreased (increased) in each of these occupations between 2001 and 2005?

> ➤ How many workers in core printing occupations are employed in industries other than printing?

> ➤ Which industries have increased (decreased) their employment in occupations specific to Design/Prepress, Print Production or Postpress activities?

The report is organized into six sections. Section I describes the source data on occupational employment, sampling procedures, and the methodological issues involved in constructing comparable industry categories from the available data for 2000, 2001, and 2005. Section II describes the types of printing-related occupations and identifies those that are core to each stage of the printing process. Section III focuses on the printing industry and eight other industry groups that were significant employers of core printing occupations in 2005. There are three additional categories that contain the remainder of printing occupational employment in manufacturing, services, and other sectors of the economy. Therefore, Section III also contains an analysis of the relative importance of these industry groups as employers for each core printing occupation. Section IV focuses on occupational earnings. It includes a description of the average earnings of workers in 2005 for each core printing occupation and an analysis of industry differences in high- and low-wage employment opportunities. Section V analyzes occupational employment growth for all industries (including printing), as well as the differences among industry groups in the patterns of growth for each core occupation. Lastly, Section VI ends the report with observations about the major findings detailed in Sections III, IV, and V.

SECTION I: DATA SOURCES ON EMPLOYMENT IN PRINTING OCCUPATIONS

This section of the report describes the sources of national occupational employment data, sampling procedures used to collect industry-specific information, and the methodological problems in making comparisons by industry and year.

Government Surveys and Employment Records

The U.S. Bureau of Labor Statistics is the source for national and industry-specific estimates of occupational employment and wages. Within the BLS, the Occupational Employment Statistics (OES) program is responsible for the sampling procedures and questionnaires that the states use in biannual surveys of establishments. The OES maintains the database on establishments, and uses these data to construct employment and wage estimates for all occupations and industries.

The OES relies on two sources of data for its estimates of the total number of workers employed in a particular occupation in each industry. One source is government (at both the federal and state levels) and the other is a nation-wide survey of establishments sampled by size and industry. A census of all federal government agencies is conducted annually by the federal Office of Management and Budget (OMB). Each state government also compiles annual data on occupational employment for non-federal government agencies within its borders. Hence, the occupational employment estimates for government agencies (federal, state, and local) and the U.S. postal service are based on data for the entire population of government establishments (excluding military occupations). For each industry, the OES uses sample data collected in surveys of establishments conducted by each state's Employment Security Agency. The most recent estimates of occupational employment for all industries that have been published by the OES at the time of this writing are for May of 2005.

Since November of 2002, the OES has conducted two biannual surveys of 200,000 establishments (in May and November). Prior to 2002, one annual survey of 400,000 establishments was conducted each year. In 1999, 2000, and 2001, the annual sample size was approximately 400,000 establishments. The occupational employment estimates for 2001 and 2005 are based on a combined sample of 1.2 million establishments collected over a three-year period. The 2005 estimates include sample data from 2003, 2004, and 2005. The 2001 employment estimates were derived from sample data collected in 1999, 2000, and 2001. Thus, occupational estimates for these two years are derived from independent samples in different periods. For that reason, all analyses of occupational employment change are based on the estimates for 2005 and 2001.[1]

Occupational Classification System

All federal government agencies that collect information on jobs use the *Standard Occupational Classification* (SOC) system developed by the Office of Management and Budget (OMB). Although this system has been the standard for all agencies since 2000, the OES began to use the SOC in 1999. Hence, national employment data on the same occupational classifications are available from 1999 to the present.

---

1 - Additional details on sampling and data collection procedures are included in the Technical Appendix on Data and Methodological Issues.

The SOC has four levels of aggregation: major and minor groups and broad and detailed occupational categories. Each occupation in the SOC belongs to a single occupational group. In all, there are 34 major occupational groups. Table 1 displays a description and the SOC code for each group.

Table 1. Major Occupational Groups

11-0000	Management Occupations
13-0000	Business and Financial Operations Occupations
15-0000	Computer and Mathematical Occupations
17-0000	Architecture and Engineering Occupations
19-0000	Life, Physical, and Social Services Occupations
21-0000	Community and Social Services Occupations
23-0000	Legal Occupations
25-0000	Education, Training, and Library Occupations
27-0000	Arts, Design, Entertainment, Sports, and Media Occupations
29-0000	Healthcare Practitioners and Technical Occupations
31-0000	Healthcare Support Occupations
33-0000	Protective Service Occupations
35-0000	Food Preparation and Serving Related Occupations
37-0000	Building and Grounds Cleaning and Maintenance Occupations
39-0000	Personal Care and Service Occupations
41-0000	Sales and Related Occupations
43-0000	Office and Administrative Support Occupations
45-0000	Farming, Fishing, and Forestry Occupations
47-0000	Construction and Extraction Occupations
49-0000	Installation, Maintenance, and Repair Occupations
51-0000	Production Occupations
53-0000	Transportation and Material Moving Occupations
55-0000	Military Specific Occupations

The major groups are divided further into 96 minor groups and 449 broad occupational categories with more than 800 detailed occupations. [2] The SOC system consists of a six-digit classification. The first two digits identify major groups. Within each group, occupations may be differentiated by as many as four digits. Summary statistics on employment for each occupational group are available for each period for major industry classifications. [3] With the exception of group 55, 'Military Specific Occupations,' employment and wage data are available for all SOC

2 - *Standard Occupational Classification Manual* (2003), p. x.

3 - Prior to 2002, the major industry classifications corresponded to the three-digit level of the SIC. From 2002 onward, the OES used the NAICS system of industry classification and occupational employment estimates are available for most 4-digit NAICS industry classifications. The technical appendix also includes details on the construction of comparable industry groups for 2001 and 2005 from the OES data.

occupational categories from 1999 to the present.

Printing Occupations in SOC Groups

Occupations that are related to printing are identified with 3 of the 22 groups (27-0000 Arts, Design, Entertainment, Sports, and Media Occupations. 43-0000 Office and Administrative Support Occupations, and 51-0000 Production Occupations). Table 2 provides description of the fourteen printing specialist occupations by occupational title and occupational group, and illustrative job titles identified with each occupational title. The descriptions and job titles are excerpted from the *Standard Occupational Classification Manual*. In addition, each occupation is identified as either exclusive to printing (S) or frequently associated but not necessarily exclusive to the printing process (R). Of these, nine are identified as occupations that involve printing tasks, no matter the industry employer. Five occupations are considered to be print-related, but, in some industries, the occupation may not signify a printing-specific process (or product). For example, cementing & gluing machine operators may be part of the process of producing a non-print product. Similarly, paper machine setters may be engaged in the manufacturing of paper products in establishments that do not perform any printing operations on these products. As for photography (and the occupations related to it), the process may be considered to be a specialization that is frequently employed in the printing process, but at least some of the time (in some industries) it is not a printing-specific occupation.

Table 2. Printing Related Occupations in the Standard Occupational Classification System

SOC code	Occupational Title and Description	Illustrative Job Titles
27-0000	Arts, Design, Entertainment, Sports, and Media Occupations	
27-1024	Graphic Designer (S) Design or create graphics to meet specific commercial or promotional needs, such as packaging, displays, or logos. May use a variety of mediums to achieve artistic or decorative effects.	Catalogue Illustrator; Graphic Artist; Layout Artist
27-3041	Editor (S) Perform variety of editorial duties, such as laying out, indexing, and revising content of written materials, in preparation for final publication.	Copy Editor; Censor; Reviewer
27-4021	Photographers (R) Photograph persons, subjects, merchandise, or other commercial products. May develop negatives and produce finished prints.	Camera Operator
43-0000	Office and Administrative Support Occupations	
43-9031	Desktop Publishers (S) Format typescript and graphic elements using computers, scanners, and software for electronic-publishing; perform image-setting and color separation operations in order to produce print-ready material.	Electronic Publisher; Electronic Typographer and Compositor
43-9081	Proofreaders and Copy Markers (S) Read transcript or proof type setup to detect and mark for correction any grammatical, typographical, or compositional errors.	Copy Reader

Table 2. Printing Related Occupations in the Standard Occupational Classification System (con't.)

SOC code	Occupational Title and Description	Illustrative Job Titles
51-0000	Production Occupations	
51-5011	Bindery Worker (S) Set up or operate binding machines that produce books and other printed materials. Includes hand bindery worker, except bookbinders.	Book Coverer; Stitching Machine Operator; Bind. Machine Operator
51-5012	Bookbinder (S) Perform highly skilled hand finishing operations, such as grooving and lettering to bind books.	Book Finisher; Book Mender
51-5021	Job Printer (S) Set-up and operate printing press, and perform prepress tasks such as photo composition, layout, plate-making, reading proof for errors and clarity of impression, and correcting imperfections.	Job Press Operator
51-5022	Prepress Technician (S) Set up and prepare material for printing presses, including compositing, typesetting, layout, paste-up, camera operator, scanning, film stripping, and photoengraving.	Compositor; Lithographer; Photoengraving Etcher
51-5023	Printing Machine Operators (S) Set up and operate various types of printing machines, such as offset, letterset, intaglio, or gravure presses or screen printers, to produce print on paper or other materials.	Bag Printer; Offset Press Operator
51-9131	Photographic Process Workers (R) Perform precision work involved in photographic processing, such as editing photographic negatives and prints, using photo-mechanical, chemical, or computerized methods.	Photographic Colorist or Finisher; Darkroom Technician
51-9132	Photographic Processing Machine Operators (R) Operate photographic processing machines, such as photographic printing machines, film developing machines, and mounting presses.	Film Printer or Processor; Reproduction Machine Loader
51-9191	Cementing and Gluing Machine Operators/Tenders (R) Operate or tend cementing and gluing machines to join items for further processing or to form a completed. Processes include joining veneer sheets into plywood; gluing paper; joining rubber and rubberized fabric parts, plastic, simulated leather, or other materials. Excludes "Shoe Machine Operators and Tenders" (51-6042)	Bonding Molder; Paper Sealer; Taper Operator
51-9196	Paper Goods Machine Setters, Operators/Tenders (R) Set up, operate, or tend paper goods machines that perform a variety of functions, such as converting, sawing, corrugating, banding, wrapping, boxing, stitching, forming, or sealing paper or paperboard sheets into products	Bag Machine Operator; Box Fabricator; Carton Forming Machine Operator

Note: (S) 100% Print-Specific; (R) Print-Related (not always printing).
Source: *Standard Occupational Classification on CD-ROM (2000)*

SECTION II: PRINTING OCCUPATIONS BY STAGE OF THE PRODUCTION PROCESS

In broad terms, occupational specializations can be distinguished by the stage of production and the sequence of tasks and specialized skills necessary to make the intermediate and final products for which the printing industries are known. Table 3 identifies the tasks and responsibilities of printing specialist occupations in relation to the three major stages of the printing production process. These are *Design & Prepress*, *Print Production*, and *Postpress/Bindery* (also referred to as *Postpress*).

The first stage of the printing process begins with the design, composition, and layout of the image to be printed (*Design & Prepress*). Along with *Graphic Designers*, editors, and proofreaders, design and prepress occupations include specialists in photographic processes, plate making and other tasks necessary to prepare the printing press for production. In some establishments, *Prepress Technicians* perform all of these operations. In others, tasks are specialized by occupation, as in the case of photography occupations.

The second stage, *Print Production*, contains those occupations that are directly involved in operating printing presses and related machinery. Included in printing press operations are paper machine setters and operators that make paper products in an integrated printing/paper product manufacturing process. *Job Printers* and *Printing Machine (Press) Operators* have responsibility for setting up printing presses, monitoring the equipment and making any necessary adjustments while the press is running. In some establishments, workers also perform routine maintenance on these machines. In addition to press operations, the *Job Printer* performs the tasks of the *Prepress Technician*, including photocomposition, layout, and plate making.

All other production jobs that involve operations that transform the printed material to a finished printed product are classified as *Postpress* work. *Bindery Workers* perform a variety of tasks necessary to turn the printed material into a finished product. In high-volume production operations, many of these tasks have been mechanized, and bindery work consists of specialized semi-skilled machine operator occupations, such as cementing and gluing machine operators. *Bookbinders* are specialists that make customized bindings, or repair and restore rare books.

Design & Prepress

Five printing-unique occupations are identified with *Design & Prepress* tasks in the printing process: *Graphic Designer, Editor, Desktop Publisher, Proofreader*, and *Prepress Technician*. Three of these are considered to be "core" to the printing production process: *Graphic Designer, Desktop Publisher*, and *Prepress Technician*. Compared to occupations identified with other stages in the production process, *Design & Prepress* occupations appear to have the greatest variation in skills and educational requirements. The jobs with relatively high educational requirements are the *Graphic Designer* and *Editor*. *Graphic Designers* are responsible for planning and creating the design and layout of images and text of such printed documents as magazines and brochures, printed material on packaging (paper, plastic or metal), apparel and textiles, and cards. *Graphic Designers* may also perform tasks identified with other printing occupations.

Table 3. Tasks and Responsibilities of Printing Occupations by Stage of the Production Process

Design & Prepress

Graphic Designers, Editors, Proofreaders & Copy Markers, Desktop Publishers	Design or create graphics for packaging, displays, or logos.
	Format typescript and graphic elements using computer software to produce publication-ready material.
	Copy-edit including layout, indexing, and revising content of written materials.
	Proof-reading of galley prints to detect and mark for correction any grammatical, typographical, or compositional errors.
Prepress Technicians, Photographers, Photographic Process and Photographic Machine Operators	Set up and prepare material for printing presses, including compositing, typesetting, layout, paste-up.
	Camera operating, scanning, film stripping.
	Photoengraving, pantograph engraving, and silk screen etching.
	Photograph and develop negatives, perform precision work involved in photographic processing (such as editing photographic negatives and prints) using photo-mechanical, chemical, or computerized methods.
	Operate photographic processing machines, such as photographic printing machines and film developing machines.
	Mounting film [or plates] on presses to produce finished prints.

Print Production

Job Printers, Printing Machine (Press) Operators, Paper Goods Machine Setters and Operators	Set type according to copy.
	Operate press to print job order, read proof for errors and clarity of impression, and correct imperfections.
	Set up or operate various types of printing machines, such as offset, letterset, intaglio, gravure, or screen presses to produce print on paper or other materials.
	Set up, operate, or tend paper goods machines that form or seal paper or paperboard sheets into products (for integrated print and paper product manufacturing).

Postpress/Bindery

Bindery Workers, Bookbinders, Cementing and Gluing Machine Operators	Set up or operate binding machines that produce books and other printed materials.
	Perform highly skilled hand finishing operations, such as grooving and lettering to bind books.
	Operate or tend cementing and gluing machines gluing paper; joining rubber and rubberized fabric parts, plastic, simulated leather, or other materials.
	Stapling, stitching, trimming, sewing, and other finishing operations.

Sources: Bureau of Labor Statistics, US Department of Labor. *Occupational Outlook Handbook, 2004-5 Edition* and *Standard Occupational Classification Manual on CD-ROM.*

The *Desktop Publisher* and the *Proofreader* are classified as Office and Administrative Support occupations. *Desktop Publisher* refers to a set of new occupations with various titles, such as Electronic Publisher, Electronic Prepress Technician, Image Designer, Typographer, Compositor or Layout Artist, and Web Publication Designer. These occupations use computers, scanners, and software for **electronic** publishing, image-setting and color separation operations. Desktop publishing occupations may include tasks of the *Graphic Designer* and incorporate many of the responsibilities that were once the sole province of the traditional (non-electronic) *Prepress Technician*. Recent advances in these technologies allow desktop publishing specialists to create an entire publication (magazine, brochure, etc.) on a computer. The resulting image shown on a video display terminal is nearly the same as the printed page. [4] With some systems, the *Desktop Publisher* (or *Graphic Designer*) sends an electronic file directly to production, where plates are made by a computer using the information in the file(s) produced by the Desktop Publisher. *Proofreaders & Copy Markers* specialize in proofing and marking copy from a preliminary printing run. These are relatively low-skill occupations that are presently being absorbed as ancillary tasks of other printing occupations. Increasingly, proofing and marking up copy are being performed by other printing-specific occupations, such as the *Prepress Technician, Desktop Publisher, Graphic Designer*, and *Job Printer*.

Prepress Technicians include a number of specializations. Technicians using hand tools, photographic and film processing equipment, typesetting machines, electronic scanners, and computers compose and layout text, graphics, drawings and photographs for each "image" or "document" to be printed. Plate making specialists use different methods to make the plates or rollers for printing presses (lithographic, gravure, flexographic, and screen) that transfer the inked image to paper, fabric, or other media. Other specializations include the use of photo-typesetting and film processing equipment.

Print Production & Press Operations

In this stage, two production occupations are unique to the printing process — the *Job Printer* and *Printing Machine Operator*. [5] *Job Printers* and *Printing Machine Operators* have responsibility for setting up printing presses, monitoring the equipment, and making any necessary adjustments while the press is running. Some operators may be responsible for monitoring several machines at the same time. In some establishments, workers in these occupations may also perform routine maintenance on these machines. In addition to press operations, the *Job Printer* performs the tasks of the *Prepress Technician*, including photocomposition, layout, and plate making. In some establishments, the *Job Printer* may be expected to operate different types of printing presses, e.g., screen printing and lithographic machines.

Postpress/Bindery

Two occupations specialize in tasks that are unique to the *Postpress/Bindery* stage of the printing process: the generic *Bindery Worker* and the specialized *Bookbinder*. All other occupations identified with *Postpress/Bindery* involve tasks and machines that may be used in other production processes as well. *Bindery Workers* perform a

---

4 - The colors that appear on the screen will not necessarily have the same tone when printing. This is why color proofing systems that generate printed copy are still necessary.

5 - In all subsequent tables and figures, the occupation "printing machine operator" is referred to as *Press Operator*.

variety of tasks, such as stitching, folding, cutting, or gluing the printed material. In some printing establishments, these tasks are performed by hand, while in other, high-volume production operations many of these tasks have been mechanized, and bindery work consists of specialized semi-skilled machine operator occupations. *Bookbinders* are specialists that make customized bindings or repair and restore rare books.

Core Printing Occupations

Of the nine occupations unique to printing, six were identified as *core occupations*. These include three *Design & Prepress* occupations, two *Print Production* occupations, and the generic *Bindery Worker* occupation (SOC 51-5011). The selected occupations include such relatively "new" occupations as the *Desktop Publisher, Job Printer*, and the computer-based *Graphic Designer*. In addition, the selection includes one traditional occupation from each stage of the printing process – *Prepress Technician, Press Operator*, and the generic *Bindery Worker* occupation.

Editors, Proofreaders, and *Bookbinders* were excluded for a number of reasons. A printed product may be a logo or company name printed on a container. For such products, editors and proofreaders are not essential to the production process. Computerization of printing processes in the prepress and production stages allows establishments outside the printing industry to perform many of the prepress tasks formerly performed by *Prepress Technicians* and proofreaders in the printing industry. As a consequence of the change in the location of prepress activity, the printing industry will have less demand for proofreaders, since these tasks are increasingly being performed by either the *Graphic Designer* or the *Desktop Publisher* in other industries who produce the final press-ready "copy" in electronic form. The new type of *Prepress Technician* ('*pre-flight*') has responsibility of checking the "virtual" proof and the *Job Printer* uses these computer files to prepare a press for a production run. As for *Postpress/Bindery* occupations, the generic *Bindery Worker* occupation includes a broad array of postpress tasks, and workers were employed in large numbers in 2000 and 2001. By contrast, only 7,660 workers were employed as a *Bookbinder* in 2005, and there were only 1,420 such jobs outside the printing industry. Due to the small number of workers and the high concentration in the printing industry, *Bookbinder* is excluded from the group of core printing occupations.

Table 4 shows the number of jobs for each printing occupation as reported in the 2005 national occupational employment estimates released by the OES. At that time, nearly 600,000 workers were employed in these occupations. *Design & Prepress* occupations accounted for 47.7%, whereas *Print Production* and *Postpress/Bindery* occupations were responsible for 52.3% of the total. The *Press Operator* had the most employment, with 192,520 jobs (32.7%). The *Graphic Designer* was the second largest, employing 178,530 workers. Even though the *Desktop Publisher* uses computers and is responsible for an electronic form of prepress, this occupation had the fewest jobs: only 29,910 workers were employed as *Desktop Publishers* in 2005.

Table 4. Employment in Core Printing Occupations, All Industries' Total, 2005

Design and Prepress Occupations		280,490 jobs	47.7%
SOC Code	Occupational Title	Employment	Percent Share, All Core Occupations
27-1024	Graphic Designer	178,530	30.4%
43-9031	Desktop Publisher (Electronic Prepress)	29,910	5.1%
51-5022	Prepress Technician	72,050	12.3%
Production and Postpress Occupations		307,430 jobs	52.3%
SOC Code	Occupational Title	Employment	Percent Share, All Core Occupations
51-5023	Press (Printing Machine) Operator	192,520	32.7%
51-5021	Job Printer	50,580	8.6%
51-5011	Bindery Worker	64,330	10.9%
Total Employment in above-listed occupations		587,920	

SECTION III: INDUSTRY DIFFERENCES IN EMPLOYMENT

This section focuses on the array of industries in which workers are employed in printing occupations. In this analysis, the most recent data on occupational employment by industry is used. The latest release of occupational employment with industry details are for May of 2005. The questions addressed in this section include:

> How much employment of **Design & Prepress** activity (as measured by employment in relevant occupations) is located outside of the printing industry?

> As measured by the employment of *Job Printers* and *Press Operators*, how much employment of **Production Printers** occurs in industries other than printing?

> For specific occupations, which industries are the most important employers?

Printing Industry Employment in Core Occupations

Obviously, "printing" is the primary product specific to the printing industry (NAICS 3231). If the industry dominated all stages of the printing production process, we would expect to find the printing industry to be the dominant employer for core occupations at each stage of the production process. Figure 1 shows the distribution of core occupational employment divided by stage of the printing process for the printing industry and all other industries. [6] The pie chart on the left depicts the distribution of employment among core occupations in the

---

6 - "Other Industries" employment was calculated by subtracting the printing industry's employment from the national total of 587,920 workers employed in core printing occupations.

printing industry. The pie chart on the right shows the shares of core occupational employment by stage of the printing process for all other industries. In comparison to the printing industry, the figure shows that "All Other Industries" had a larger overall share of employment in core printing occupations (56.7%). Moreover, looking at the distribution of employment by stage in the production process, Figure 1 shows that 211,150 of the 333,350 workers employed in other industries were in ***Design & Prepress*** occupations. By comparison, the printing industry employed only 69,340 workers in ***Design & Prepress*** occupations. In the printing industry, ***Production Printers*** dominate employment, accounting for 53.3% of the 254,570 workers in all core printing occupations within the industry. Still, in 2005, there were nearly as many ***Production Printers*** (107,410) employed in other industries as in the printing industry. Lastly, *Bindery Workers* — the occupation representative of the post-production stage — were a minority of the workforce in both the printing industry and all other industries combined.

Figure 1. Printing and All Other Industries' Employment Shares of Core Occupations by Stage of Printing Process, 2005

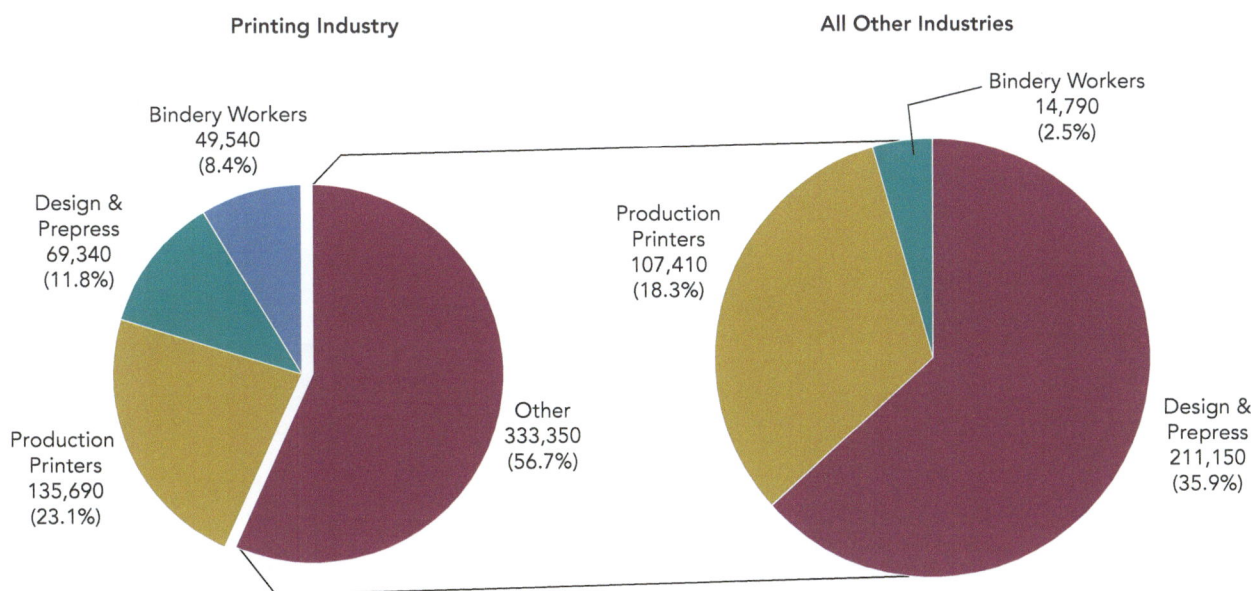

Figure 2 shows the printing industry's employment for each core occupation and the number of jobs in all other industries. The figure shows the number of jobs and the relative shares of occupational employment in the printing industry and "All Other Industries". Among ***Design & Prepress*** occupations, the printing industry dominates employment in only one occupation, *Prepress Technician*. Moreover, in 2005, the number of *Prepress Technicians* employed by the printing industry exceeded the industry's employment in the occupations of *Graphic Designer, Desktop Publisher*, and *Job Printer*. The printing industry employed 11% of all *Graphic Designers* and 25% of all *Desktop Publishers*. With respect to ***Production Printers***, the printing industry employed more than half of all *Press Operators* and nearly two-thirds of all *Job Printers*, with three *Press Operators* for each worker employed as a *Job Printer*. In all other industries, there were many more workers employed as *Press Operators* than as *Job Printers*, with five workers in the *Press Operator* occupation for each worker employed as a *Job Printer*. Lastly, in 2005, there were 49,540 *Bindery Workers* employed in the printing industry in 2005, accounting for 77% of all employment in this occupation.

Figure 2. Employment in Each Core Printing Occupation, Printing Industry and All Other Industries, 2005

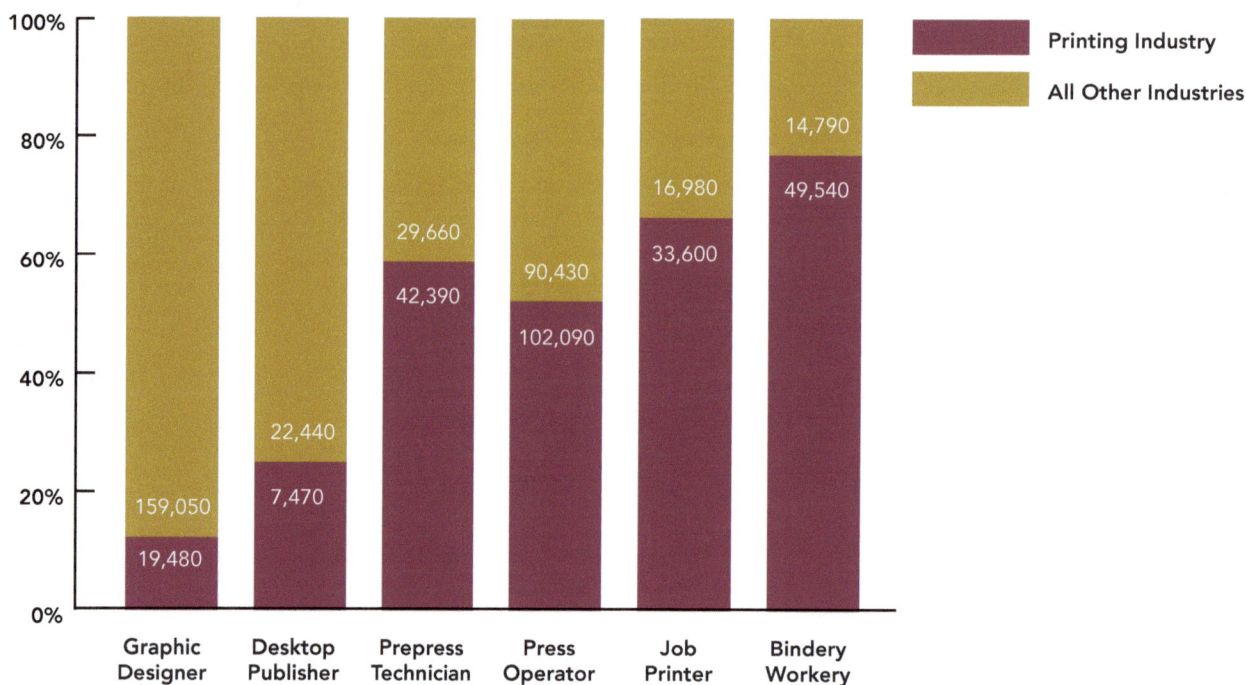

All Other Industries

The "All Other Industries" category consists of nine groups of related industries and three groups in which industries are related only by sector. The groups were constructed using the NAICS and SIC industry codes available from the OES occupational data. [7] In 2005, of the 333,350 workers who were employed in core printing occupations outside the printing industry, all but 490 jobs were identified with one of these industry groups. Table 5 provides a description of each industry group and the acronym that will be used to identify the group in all subsequent figures and tables. With the exception of the **NEC** category, each group employed at least 1.0% of all workers in a specific core printing occupation. In the manufacturing sector, there are two industry groups — **Apparel/Textiles** and **Package** — with special requirements for print. A third manufacturing category, **Other Mfg**, includes all other manufacturing industries. Some industries in the **Other Mfg** category have unique printing requirements (e.g., food processing, cigarette manufacturing), but there were too few workers employed in printing occupations by these industries to warrant a separate group.

The non-manufacturing sectors include service industries, wholesale and retail trade, government, and construction and utilities. **W&R Trade** includes all retail stores, wholesalers, and direct selling establishments. **Govnt**

7 - A detailed description of the NAICS and SIC industry classifications belonging to each group is included in the technical appendix.

includes the administration of federal, state, and local governments. **Govnt** does *not* include employment in public education (primary and secondary schools or state and city colleges), publicly provided (or owned) health services, utilities, transportation, or the military. [8] The **Educ & Health** group includes both service and manufacturing industries. The industries that manufacture pharmaceuticals, medical equipment, and supplies are classified as "Health Products". Employment in these industries and the industries that provide health services (e.g., hospitals and offices of medical professionals and other service providers) are identified as **Health**, while employment in primary and secondary schools, colleges and other educational services is classified as **Educ**. Thus, the **Educ & Health** group is comprised of all industries that provide education and health services or products. Four industry groups are comprised solely of specialized service industries — **Prof & Biz, FIRE, Publish** and **Telecom**. All other services, including entertainment, personal services, transportation and travel services, membership organizations and other non-profit associations, are classified as **Other Serv**. As in the case of **Other Mfg**, industries in the **Other Serv** category include some industries with unique requirements, such as transportation, where there were too few jobs to warrant separate classifications. Lastly, the **NEC** category includes all other industries with any employment in a printing occupation. Even though such industries as agriculture and mining belong in the **NEC** category, the only sectors that the OES identifies as employing any workers in a core printing occupation were in construction and utilities industries.

With respect to differences in the use of print, screen printing of fabrics and apparel and printed decals on accessories characterize the use of print by **Apparel/Textiles**. The **Package** industries make the bags, boxes and containers, and flexible wrapping materials that are used to "package" other products. Print may be part of the process of making the packaging itself, particularly for flexible packaging, paper bags and boxes. The print on the package may identify the contents, show product logos, or display images of the contents. In addition, some print on packaging materials is simply decorative (e.g., wrapping paper depicting holiday scenes, baby or wedding showers, birthdays, and other motifs). [9]

Publish includes print-based publishers of magazines, newspapers, and books (including musical scores). Like **Apparel/ Textiles** and **Package**, printing is an intrinsic attribute of all products of the **Publish** group. [10] Prior to 1997, the U.S. industry classifications system defined print-based publishing industries as belonging to the manufacturing sector. In recent years, the production of printed publications is likely to take place in a separate establishment from the place where the publications are generated by writers, artists, photographers, and graphic designers, and would therefore be classified as belonging to the printing industry. Still, some publishing establishments combine the preparation of the print-based publication with their own print production operations.

The publishing industries are likely to have a greater need for specialists in *electronic* prepress, image design,

8 - Employment in the U.S. Armed Services is not reported in the OES data. Employment in all other services provided by government agencies are assigned to comparable industries in which such services are provided by the private sector.

9 - Package excludes those industries for which there are no comparable SIC/NAICS classifications. The industries identified with metal containers are comparable only at the 5-6 digit NAICS and 4-5digit SIC. With 3-digit SIC and 4-digit NAICS, only the industries that include glass, paper-based, and plastic packaging are comparable.

10 - All non-print publishing such as software and internet publishing is excluded from the group.

Table 5. Characteristics of Industry Groups

Industry Group	Acronym	Description of Industries	
Containers and flexible wrapping	Package	Paper, plastic and glass containers; flexible wrapping; envelopes.	
Textiles, apparel, footwear and leather goods	Apparel / Textiles	Textile fabrics, clothing, shoes, & leather goods.	
Newspaper, book and directory publishers	Publish	All print-based publishing. Excludes software and publication in other media.	
Professional and business services	Prof & Biz	Three clusters of services: Adv & Design, R&D / Other Prof and Mgmt / Biz Support services.	
		Adv & Design	Advertising, graphic design and other design services.
		R&D / Other Prof	Scientific research and product development services; other professional services including law, accounting, architecture and engineering, software design, computer programming and data processing services.
		Mgmt / Biz Support	Mgmt/HQ consists of national and regional headquarters and holding companies. Biz Support includes management consulting and other administrative services and support services such as equipment maintenance and repair, building maintenance, and security.
Heath products and services, education services	Educ & Health	Hospitals, doctors' offices, other health services, drugs, medical equipment and supplies; primary and secondary schools, colleges and universities, vocational training and other educational services.	
Wholesale and retail trade	W&R Trade	Distributors and retailers, including direct selling.	
Finance, insurance, and real estate	FIRE	Banking, securities and commodities; insurance; real estate agencies.	
Telecommunication industries	Telecom	Cable and other subscription programming, television and radio broadcasting, wired telecommunication services.	
Federal, state, and local government administration	Govnt	Federal, state and local government administration. Excludes publicly provided health, education, social services and the military.	
Other manufacturing	Other Mfg	Manufacturing industries, excluding industries in PRINT, Apparel/ Textiles, Package, and Educ & Health.	
Other services	Other Serv	All other services, excluding industries in Telecom, Prof & Biz, Educ & Health, Publish, and W&R Trade.	
Misc. Industries	NEC	Construction and utilities.	

Notes: Each industry group is composed of a comparable set of industries at 3-digit SIC and 4-digit NAICS classifications. The groups are inclusive of all industries with any employment in a core printing occupation in 2001 or 2005.

composition, and layout. These jobs constitute the desktop publishing occupation. Recent advances in these technologies allow desktop publishing specialists to create an entire publication (magazine, brochure, etc.) on a computer. In addition, some systems combine digitized graphic designs as well as text-based publications. Ergo, both the *Desktop Publisher* and the *Graphic Designer* can transmit an electronic file directly to a production facility that may be located elsewhere.[11]

Like **Publish**, the **Telecom** industries have particular requirements for graphic design and desktop publishing. Since the industries include cable and television programming and wired and wireless telecommunication services, workers in certain "printing" occupations may be employed to produce displays, text, documents, graphics, etc. that are not "printed" by the industry itself but can be printed by the consumer using these services.

Three other service industry groups with specialized requirements for design and/or print production are **FIRE**, **Educ & Health**, and **W&R Trade**. While these industries may have previously relied on the printing industry for both the layout of a design and the production of printed materials, the recent development of computer-generated graphics and publishing software allows these industries to take on (or in-source) at least some portion of the *Design & Prepress* stage of the printing production process. Governments (**Govnt**) have other needs for specialized printed materials (e.g., forms), some of which may be designed and printed in-house by a government agency.

The **Prof & Biz** group includes all business services and all professional services with the exception of educational and health service professions. For 2005, occupational employment in the **Prof & Biz** group is divided among three major industry clusters: **Adv & Design**, **R&D/Other Prof**, and **Mgmt/Biz Support**. For most figures and tables that display 2005 data by industry groups, the three clusters will be identified as separate groups. For any particular figure or table, there can be as many as twelve groups of related industries (including **PRINT**) and three heterogeneous classifications. Employment totals for the **Prof & Biz** group are computed as the sum of employment in these clusters.

Figure 3 shows the 2005 distribution of employment in all core printing occupations by each industry group (and related clusters) in the 'Other Industries' category. [12] Taken together, these industry groups were responsible for 56.7% of all employment in core printing occupations in 2005. The industry groups with at least 5% of the workforce employed in core printing occupations outside the **PRINT** industry are shown in the pie chart on the left. Each of these groups is considered to be major employer of workers in core printing occupations. Four industry groups and the three clusters in the **Prof & Biz** group are thereby identified. In comparison to other industry groups shown in the figure, the **Publish** industries employed more workers in core printing occupations than any of the industry groups shown in the figure (with the exception of printing) with 86,540 workers (26.0% of the

11 - With electronic prepress, the plates used by a printing press may be generated from a computer image transmitted to the production site by a specialist in computerized graphic design and composition.

12 - In 2005, less than 0.1% of all employment in core printing occupations could not be assigned to one of these industry groups (490 jobs). For each core printing occupation, the unassigned job counts were as follows: *Graphic Designer* (40), *Desktop Publisher* (120), *Prepress Technician* (100), *Press Operator* (110), *Job Printer* (70), and *Bindery Worker* (50). The Technical Appendix contains a discussion of the procedures used to reduce the 18,000 jobs that initially lacked an industry assignment (in a 4-digit NAICS classification) to 490 cases.

'Other Industries' total). **Package**, **W&R Trade**, and **Other Mfg** were fourth, fifth, and sixth respectively in core printing occupational employment. Together, these three industry groups employed 80,110 workers, or 24% of the jobs outside of the **PRINT** industry.

Separately, each cluster within the **Prof & Biz** group was a major employer, with **Adv & Design**, **Mgmt/Biz Support**, and **R&D/Other Prof** responsible for 20.0%, 8.6%, and 6.3% respectively of all jobs in core printing occupations identified with the industry groups shown in the figure. Together, this combination of industries (**Prof & Biz**) was responsible for 34.9% of all employment in core printing occupations in the 'Other Industries' category. Thus, with 116,320 workers, the **Prof & Biz** group, in its entirety, employed more workers in core printing occupations in 2005 than did the **Publish** group.

The pie chart on the right shows the contributions of industry groups that were minor employers with respect to core printing occupations (defined as having less than 5% share of all such jobs outside the **PRINT** industry). In combination, **Educ & Health**, **Apparel/Textiles**, **Govnt**, **Telecom**, and **FIRE**, contributed 39,730 jobs for 11.9% of the total in 'Other Industries'. Of the remaining jobs, 9,590 (2.9%) were found in **Other Serv** (the service industries not included in any of the five groups of related service industries — **Educ & Health**, **FIRE**, **Prof & Biz**, **Publish**, and **Telecom**). Only 570 jobs (0.2%) were identified with the construction and utilities industries in the residual **NEC** category.

Figure 3. 'Other Industries' Employment in Core Printing Occupations by Industry Group, 2005

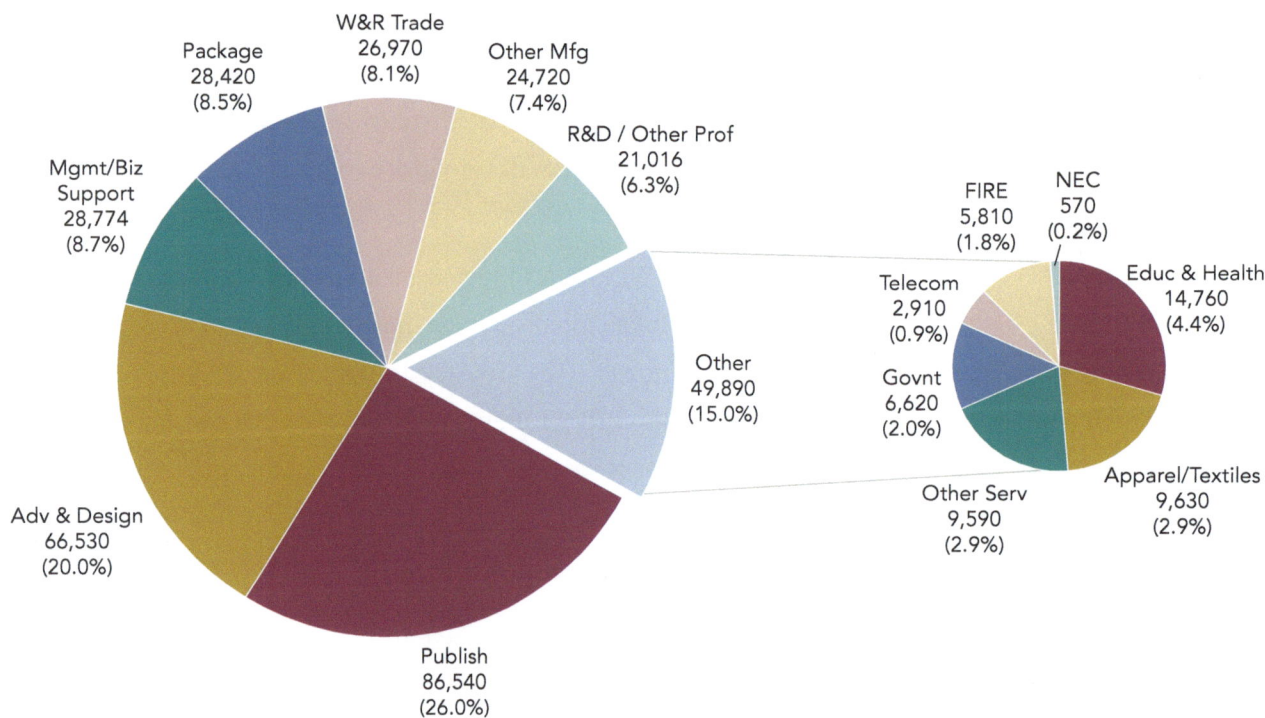

Prof & Biz = Adv & Design + Mgmt / Biz Support + R&D / Other Prof = 116,320 (35.1%)

PRINTING OCCUPATIONAL EMPLOYMENT, HIGH-WAGE JOBS,
& INDUSTRY SOURCES OF GROWTH – 2001 TO 2005

The industry groups (including **PRINT**) have substantial differences in the number and type of jobs related to the ***Design & Prepress*** stage. Outside the **PRINT** industry, the importance of ***Production Printers*** (*Job Printers* and *Press Operators*) and post-production (***Postpress/Bindery***) occupations varies greatly among industry groups. The analysis of employment patterns by stage of the printing production process that follows focuses on the industry distribution of employment for specific occupations in 2005. For the occupations of *Graphic Designer* and *Desktop Publisher*, the **PRINT** industry is not the dominant employer, and the figures showing the industry group distributions of employment for these occupations include **PRINT**. Thus, the industry group shares in Figures 4 and 5 represent percentages of employment in all industries. For the four other core occupations (*Prepress Technician, Press Operator, Job Printer*, and *Bindery Worker*), **PRINT** is the dominant industry employer. Employment in **PRINT** is therefore excluded from Figures 6, 7, and 9, which show industry distributions for these occupations. This allows a visual comparison of the differences among other industry groups. With **PRINT** excluded, the employment share in all other industry groups of *Prepress Technicians, Press Operators, Job Printers*, and *Bindery Workers* was 41.1%, 46.9%, 33.5%, and 22.9% respectively.

Graphic Designers

As discussed in previous sections of this report, the core ***Design & Prepress*** occupations — *Graphic Designer, Desktop Publisher*, and *Prepress Technician* — differ not only in the skills and technology used but also in the extent of employment (and growth) that has taken place outside the printing industry.

Figure 4 shows the industry group distribution of employment for *Graphic Designers* in 2005. Like Figure 3, the pie chart on the left represents major employers (each contributing 5% or more), while the chart on the right shows employment for minor employers (industry groups that contribute less than 5% of the total). Of the 178,490 *Graphic Designers* with an identifiable industry employer in 2005, the **Adv & Design** cluster was, by far, the largest employer of *Graphic Designers*, with 48,270 jobs (27.0% of the total). The second largest employer of *Graphic Designers*, **Publish**, accounted for only 25,440 jobs (14.3%), followed by the **PRINT** industry with 19,480 *Graphic Designers* (10.9%). The **PRINT** industry employed more *Graphic Designers* than each of the four remaining major employers — **R&D/Other Prof** (9.8%), **W&R Trade** (9.0%), **Mgmt/Biz Support** (7.6%), and **Other Mfg** (6.1 %).

Along with two heterogeneous industry categories (**Other Serv** and **NEC**), six industry groups were minor employers of *Graphic Designers*. Taken together, these groups of closely related industries — **Educ & Health, Telecom, FIRE, Apparel/Textiles, Package**, and **Govnt** — employed 19,940 *Graphic Designers* (11.2% of the total). Two of the three miscellaneous categories — **Other Serv** and **NEC** — were responsible for employing only 7,450 *Graphic Designers* (4.2%). [13] Excluding all three miscellaneous categories (**Other Mfg, Other Serv** and **NEC**), the ten industry groups that represented closely related clusters of industries were responsible for 160,180 jobs, or 89.7% of all employment, for *Graphic Designers* in 2005.

13 - *Graphic Designer* is the only occupation with employment counts for industries in the **NEC** category.

Figure 4. Employment of Graphic Designers by Industry Group, 2005

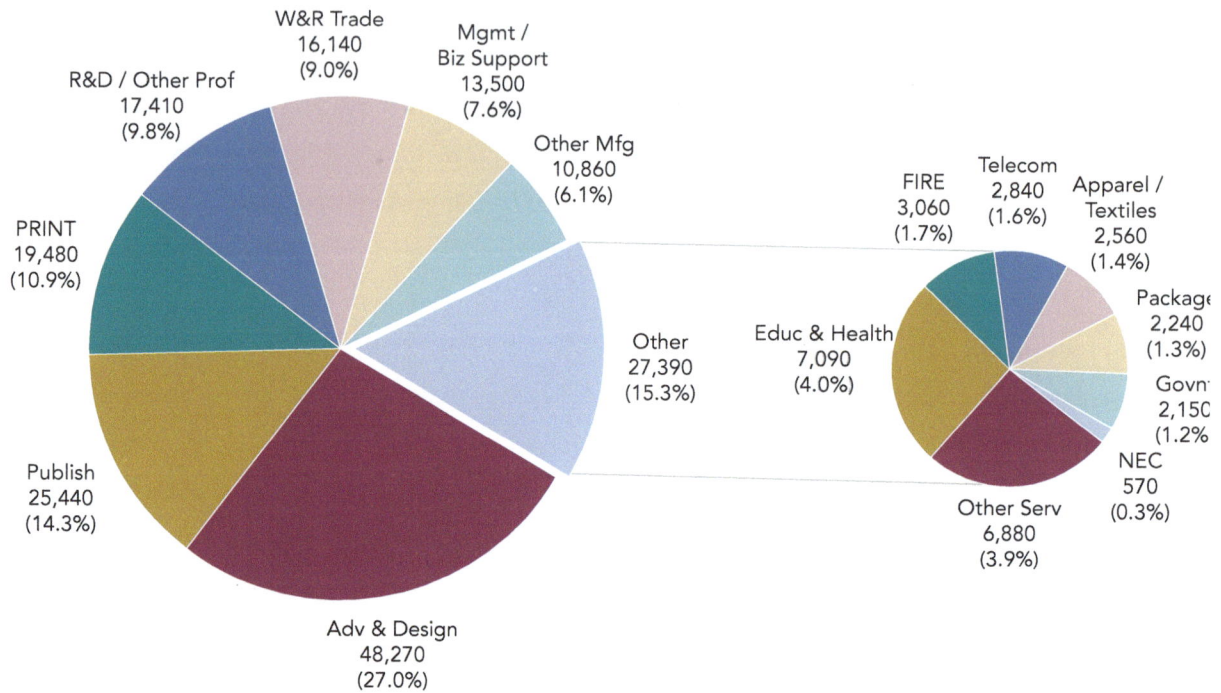

W&R Trade
16,140
(9.0%)

Mgmt /
Biz Support
13,500
(7.6%)

R&D / Other Prof
17,410
(9.8%)

Other Mfg
10,860
(6.1%)

FIRE
3,060
(1.7%)

Telecom
2,840
(1.6%)

Apparel /
Textiles
2,560
(1.4%)

PRINT
19,480
(10.9%)

Package
2,240
(1.3%)

Other
27,390
(15.3%)

Educ & Health
7,090
(4.0%)

Govnt
2,150
(1.2%)

Publish
25,440
(14.3%)

NEC
570
(0.3%)

Other Serv
6,880
(3.9%)

Adv & Design
48,270
(27.0%)

Prof & Biz = Adv & Design + Mgmt / Biz Support + R&D / Other Prof = 79,180 (44.4%)

Figure 5. Employment in Desktop Publishing Occupations by Industry Group, 2005

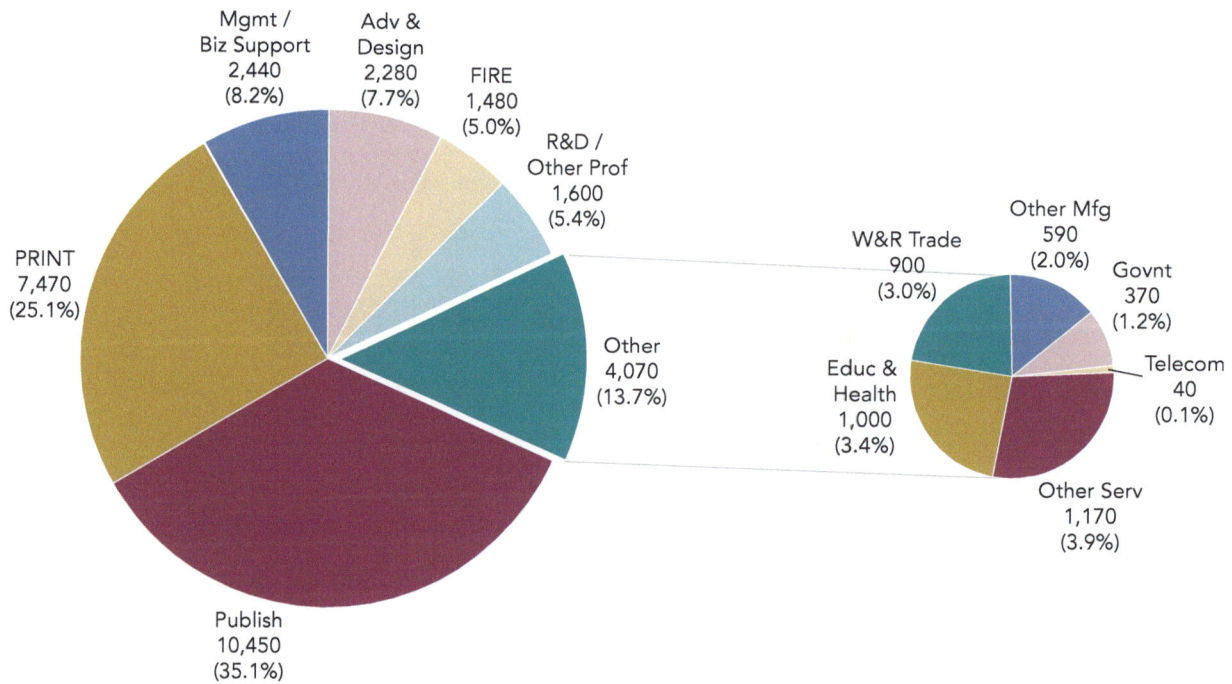

Mgmt /
Biz Support
2,440
(8.2%)

Adv &
Design
2,280
(7.7%)

FIRE
1,480
(5.0%)

R&D /
Other Prof
1,600
(5.4%)

Other Mfg
590
(2.0%)

W&R Trade
900
(3.0%)

Govnt
370
(1.2%)

PRINT
7,470
(25.1%)

Other
4,070
(13.7%)

Telecom
40
(0.1%)

Educ &
Health
1,000
(3.4%)

Publish
10,450
(35.1%)

Other Serv
1,170
(3.9%)

Prof & Biz = Adv & Design + Mgmt / Biz Support + R&D / Other Prof = 6,320 (21.2%)

Desktop Publishers

In 2005, only 29,910 workers were employed in desktop publishing occupations nationally. Of that total, 29,790 jobs were identified with specific industries. As Figure 5 indicates, the **Publish** group employed the greatest number of *Desktop Publishers*. With 10,450 workers (35.1% of the total), the **Publish** group employed more *Desktop Publishers* than all three clusters of the **Prof & Biz** group taken together (6,320 workers, 21.2%), and had more workers in this occupation than the **PRINT** industry (7,470 workers, 25.1%). The number of *Desktop Publishers* employed in **PRINT** also exceeded the jobs in **Mgmt/Biz Support** (2,440 or 8.2%), **Adv & Design** (2,280 or 7.7%), and **R&D/Other Prof** (1,600 or 5.49%). In combination, the **Publish** and **PRINT** industry groups employed 17,920 *Desktop Publishers*, for 60.2% of all such jobs. If desktop publishing jobs indicate the extent of electronic prepress activity among industries, then the two largest traditional producers of printed materials appear to be the dominant users of this prepress method in 2005.

In all, minor employers were responsible for 13.7% of all desktop publishing jobs. Among minor employers, there were four industry groups comprised of related industries. Together, **Educ & Health**, **W&R Trade**, **Telecom**, and **Govnt** contributed 2,310 jobs (7.8%). The other 1,760 (5.9%) were employed by industries in the **Other Serv** and **Other Mfg** groups. Three groups — **Package**, **Apparel/Textiles**, and **NEC** — employed no *Desktop Publishers* in 2005.

Prepress Technicians in Other Industries

Even though the majority (58.9%) of *Prepress Technicians* was employed in the **PRINT** industry in 2005, there were more *Prepress Technicians* employed in other industries than *Desktop Publishers* (29,560 versus 22,320 workers, respectively). Figure 6 shows the distribution of *Prepress Technicians* among all industry groups except the **PRINT** industry. Among these industries, the **Publish** group was, by far, the largest employer of *Prepress Technicians*, accounting for 58.7% of all jobs with 17,350 technicians employed. Three other groups of related industries were also major employers of *Prepress Technicians* – **Package**, **Adv & Design**, and **Mgmt/Biz Support**. In all, these three industry groups employed 7,430 technicians –25.1% of all such jobs outside the **PRINT** industry. Moreover, in comparison to employment in the other industries shown in the figure, the jobs in the *Prepress Technician* occupation were concentrated in these four major industry groups. Together, these four groups (**Publish**, **Package**, **Adv & Design**, and **Mgmt/Biz Support**) employed 83.8% of all *Prepress Technicians*.

All three industry clusters in the **Prof & Biz** group were major employers of *Graphic Designers* and *Desktop Publishers* in 2005, but this was not the case for *Prepress Technicians*. Instead, the **R&D/Other Prof** cluster was one of nine minor employers, employing only 690 *Prepress Technicians*. Of the eight industry groups classified as minor employers, seven consisted of related industries (**W&R Trade**, **R&D/Other Prof**, **Educ & Health**, **Govnt**, **FIRE**, **Apparel/Textiles**, and **Telecom**). In all, these groups employed 3,030 *Prepress Technicians*, for 10.3% of all such jobs outside the **PRINT** industry. **Other Serv** employed another 300 *Prepress Technicians* (1.0%). Even though there were as few as 10 *Prepress Technicians* in a particular industry group (**Telecom**), all industry groups (except those in the **NEC** category) were involved in such traditional prepress operations as layout, composition, and preparation of plates/film necessary in preparing press-ready materials for production.

Figure 6. Other Industries' Employment of Prepress Technicians by Industry Group, 2005

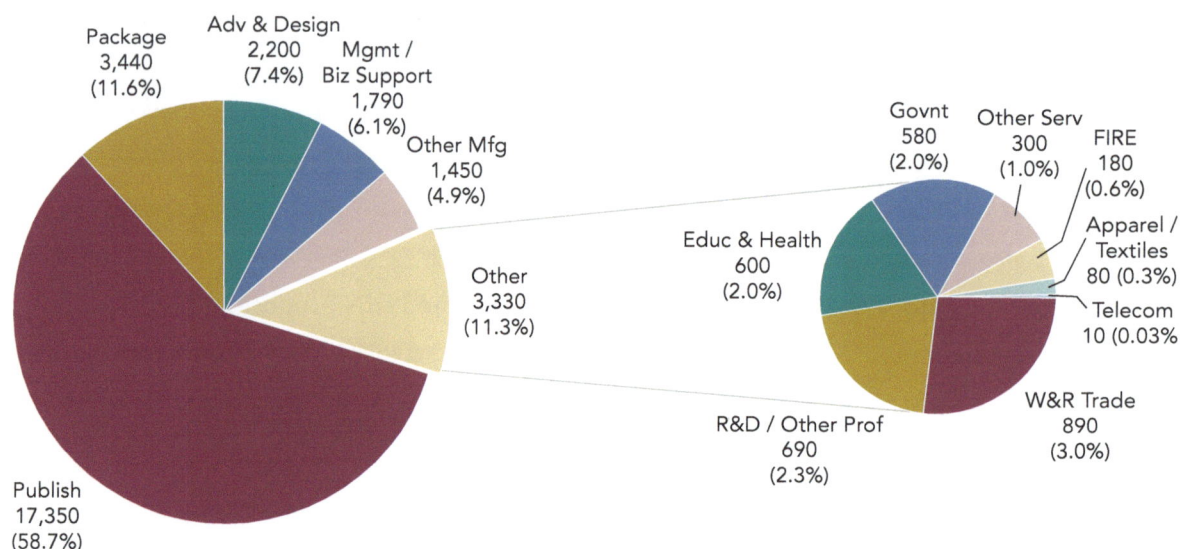

Package 3,440 (11.6%)
Adv & Design 2,200 (7.4%)
Mgmt / Biz Support 1,790 (6.1%)
Other Mfg 1,450 (4.9%)
Other 3,330 (11.3%)
Publish 17,350 (58.7%)

Govnt 580 (2.0%)
Other Serv 300 (1.0%)
FIRE 180 (0.6%)
Apparel / Textiles 80 (0.3%)
Telecom 10 (0.03%)
Educ & Health 600 (2.0%)
R&D / Other Prof 690 (2.3%)
W&R Trade 890 (3.0%)

Prof & Biz = Adv & Design + Mgmt / Biz Support + R&D / Other Prof = 4,680 (15.8%)

Production Printers

The *Job Printer* and *Press Operator* are the two occupations in the ***Production Printer*** category. In 2005, there were 243,100 ***Production Printers*** in all industries. Of that number, 242,920 were identified with specific industries. The **PRINT** industry alone employed 135,690, accounting for 55.9% of all industry-assigned ***Production Printers***. Excluding the jobs in the **PRINT** industry, there were still 107,230 ***Production Printers*** employed in other industries. Figure 7 shows the number of ***Production Printers*** divided among the industry groups in the 'Other Industries' category. The figure shows that all industry groups (except **NEC**) and each of the three industry clusters within the **Prof & Biz** group employed ***Production Printers*** in 2005 to some extent.

Among the eight major employers of ***Production Printers*** outside the **PRINT** industry, only three industry groups have been engaged in making a printed product for decades. Publishers of newspapers and magazines and producers of bags, boxes, and other packaging have been important print-producing industries for decades. Similarly, manufacturers of apparel and textiles have used various printing methods to apply images on fabric. While **Apparel/Textiles** is only the seventh of eight industry groups with at least 5% of the workers employed in ***Production Printer*** occupations, the **Publish** and **Package** industry groups were the first and second largest employers outside of the **PRINT** industry. Together, these three industry groups employed 55,480 ***Production Printers*** – more than half (51.7%) of all such jobs outside the **PRINT** industry. Even so, there were three industry groups not particularly noteworthy for printed products that were also major employers of ***Production Printers*** in 2005. The **Prof & Biz** group alone employed 10.6% of ***Production Printers*** outside the **PRINT** industry. In combination, **Prof & Biz**, **Other Mfg**, and **W&R Trade** employed 40,910 ***Production Printers*** (38.2%).

Of the 6,236 ***Production Printers*** employed by industry groups in the "minor" employer category (represented

Figure 7. Other Industries' Employment of Production Printers by Industry Group, 2005

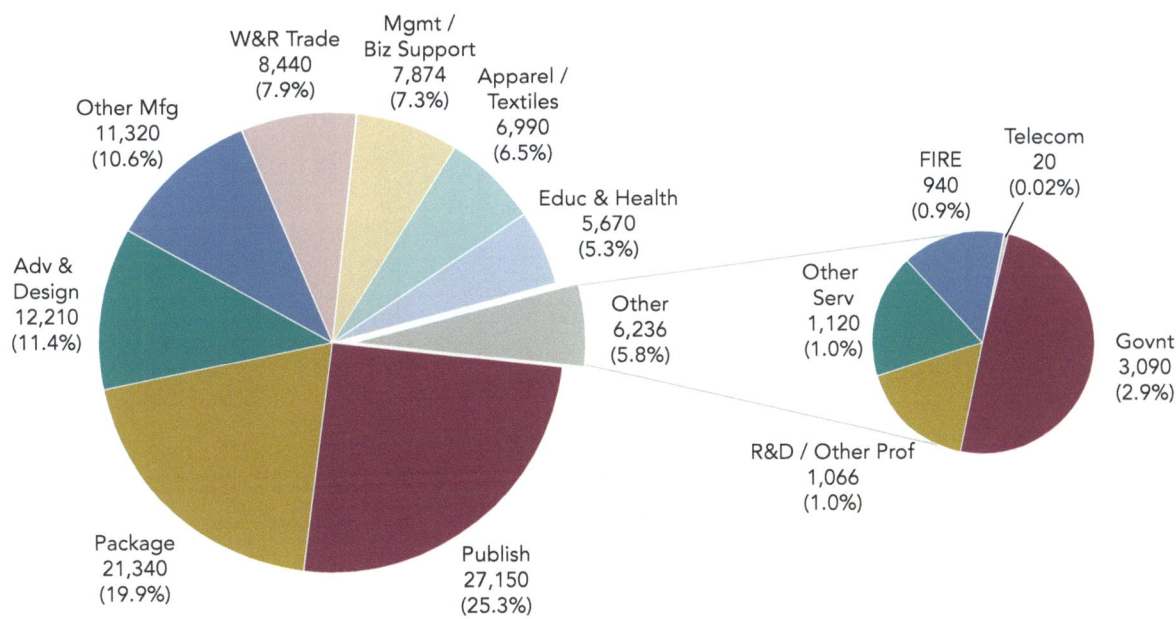

Prof & Biz = Adv & Design + Mgmt / Biz Support + R&D / Other Prof = 21,150 (19.7%)

in Figure 7 by the pie chart on the right), all but those employed in **Govnt** (3,090 jobs, 2.9%) were employed in industry groups that are not considered to be traditional print producers. Still, the traditional print-producing industries employed most of the *Production Printers* in 2005. Including the **PRINT** industry, 191,170 *Production Printers* (78.4% of all industry-assigned workers) were employed in so-called traditional print-producing industries (**Publish**, **Package**, and **Apparel/Textiles**). For workers in the *Press Operator* or *Job Printer* occupation, setting up and operating various types of printing machinery are the main responsibilities. In addition, the *Job Printer* performs the tasks of the *Prepress Technician*, including photocomposition, layout, and plate making. Only 20.8% of all *Production Printers* were employed as *Job Printers* in 2005.

Figure 8 shows the employment of *Production Printers* divided between the *Job Printer* and the *Press Operator* occupation for each industry group. The industry groups are arrayed left to right, from the largest employer of *Production Printers* (**PRINT**) to the smallest (**Telecom**). Note that the two largest employers of *Production Printers* as a whole — **PRINT** and **Publish** — were also the two largest employers of *Job Printers*. No employment data on *Job Printers* or *Press Operators* were reported for the industries in the **NEC** category.

In both the **Print** and **Publish** industry groups, *Job Printers* constituted 24.8% and 28.1%, respectively, of *Production Printers*. In **Educ & Health**, **Other Serv**, and **FIRE** groups, the *Job Printer* occupation was also relatively more important, with 30.7%, 28.6%, and 26.6%, respectively of the *Production Printers* employed in these industry groups. In **Apparel/Textiles** and **Package**, the *Job Printer* constituted only a small share of the industry groups' employment of *Production Printers*, with 0.9%, and 2.5%, respectively.[14]

14 - There were no *Job Printers* employed by **Telecom** in 2005.

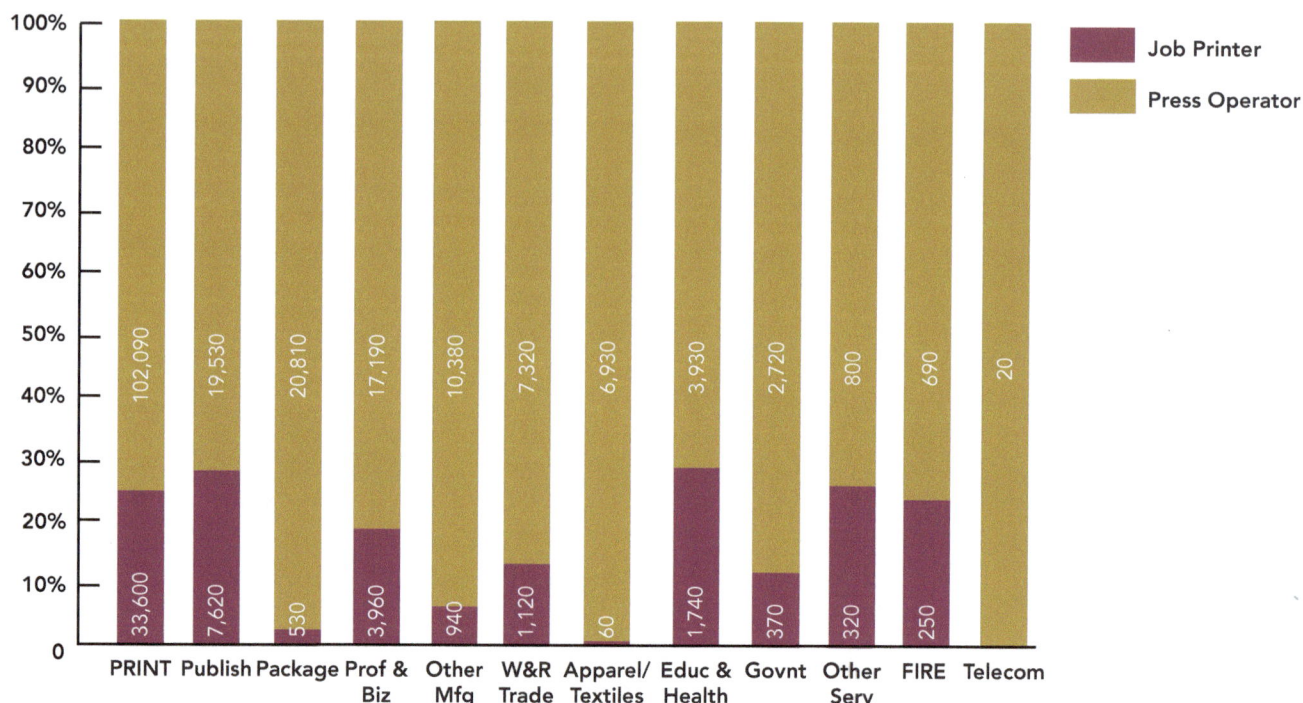

Figure 8. Employment of Press Operators and Job Printers by Industry Group, 2005

Bindery Workers in Other Industries

In 2005, 64,330 workers were employed in the *Bindery Worker* occupation. Of that total, all but 50 jobs were assigned to a specific industry. The **PRINT** industry was the largest employer of *Bindery Workers*, accounting for 49,540 jobs, which was 77.1% of the total industry-specific employment identified for that occupation. Thus, there were only 14,740 employed in other industry groups. Figure 9 shows the number of workers in this occupation for each industry group except the **PRINT** industry. As was the case for *Production Printers*, the **Publish** industry group is the largest employer of *Bindery Workers* outside the **PRINT** industry, with 41.7% of the total (6,150 jobs). While **Mgmt/Biz Support** and **Adv & Design** were the second and third largest employers, the combined employment (including **R&D/Other Prof**) of the **Prof & Biz** group was responsible for 4,990 jobs (33.9%). The **Package** group was the only other major employer of *Bindery Workers* outside of printing, accounting for 9.5% of all such jobs with 1,400 workers.

As in the case of the *Desktop Publisher* occupation, *Bindery Workers* are strongly associated with printing books and magazines, as these are documents that require binding. Therefore, in the **Apparel/Textiles** group, where the use of print is clearly unrelated to these types of print products, no workers were employed in the *Desktop Publisher* or *Bindery Worker* occupations. In addition to **Apparel/Textiles**, there were no jobs for *Bindery Workers* in the **Telecom** industries. All other industry groups that employed *Production Printers* also employed *Bindery Workers*, indicating that some portion of the printed output produced by these industries appears in the form of a book, pamphlet, or magazine.

Figure 9. Other Industries' Employment of Bindery Workers by Industry Group, 2005

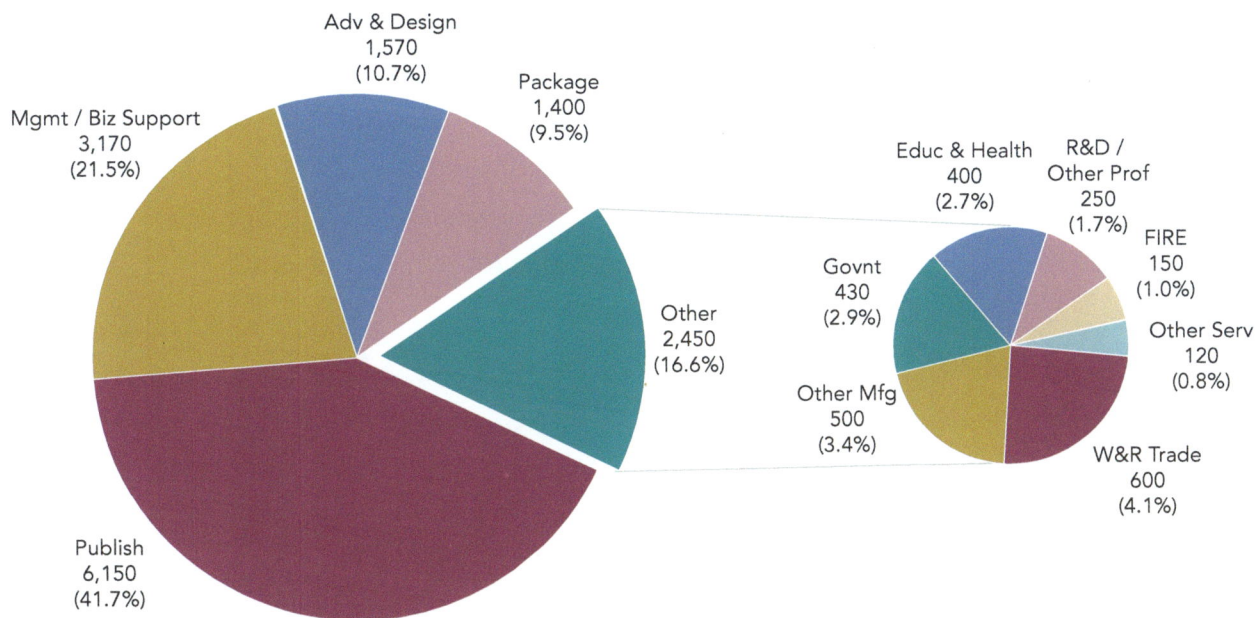

Adv & Design
1,570
(10.7%)

Package
1,400
(9.5%)

Mgmt / Biz Support
3,170
(21.5%)

Educ & Health
400
(2.7%)

R&D /
Other Prof
250
(1.7%)

FIRE
150
(1.0%)

Govnt
430
(2.9%)

Other
2,450
(16.6%)

Other Serv
120
(0.8%)

Other Mfg
500
(3.4%)

W&R Trade
600
(4.1%)

Publish
6,150
(41.7%)

Prof & Biz = Adv & Design + Mgmt / Biz Support + R&D / Other Prof = 4,990 (33.9%)

SECTION IV: INDUSTRY DIFFERENCES IN EARNINGS OF WORKERS IN CORE PRINTING OCCUPATIONS

Occupational differences in wages can be attributed to a number of factors. Generally speaking, occupations that require a college education are likely to pay higher wages than those that do not. Even when occupations do not differ in their formal education requirements, skills learned through apprenticeship or on-the-job training also explain occupation-specific differences in wages. Thus, occupations with specific skills and experience are expected to pay higher wages than entry-level occupations that require little or no training.

External market conditions are a second factor. If the demand for workers with specific skills and/or education is greater than the available supply and employers perceive there to be a "shortage", then wages may be higher as a result of competition among employers who may "bid" against one another for workers with the required skills.

Internal labor market structures are a third factor. In establishments with seniority rules, [15] workers who have more years of experience are paid higher wages than workers in the same occupation who have less experience. As a result, industries with a relatively older, more senior workforce are likely to have higher average wages. Moreover, since seniority rules often apply to layoffs in certain industries, particularly for production jobs in the manufacturing sector, wages may by relatively high because the workers who are still employed in these occupations are likely to be the most experienced and have the greatest seniority. Thus, for the same occupation, earnings are likely to vary by industry as well.

The following research questions are addressed in this section:

➤ Which occupations have the highest (lowest) wages?

➤ How large is the difference between the highest- and lowest-paid workers in each printing occupation?

➤ Which industries have more high-wage jobs in specific occupations?

➤ Which industries tend to pay lower wages?

Table 6 shows the average earnings for each core occupation by industry group. In the table, industry groups are ordered from top to bottom by overall employment in all core printing occupations. Thus, for example, there are more workers employed in core printing occupations in the **Adv & Design** cluster of industries than in the **Package** group, or any other industry group listed below that row. The last row of the table presents the national (all-industries) average wage for each occupation. For each industry group where the average earnings of an occupation were higher than the all-industries average, the amount is shown in red.

For a particular occupation, the gap between an industry's average and the national average may differ by only a few dollars. In **FIRE**, for example, *Desktop Publishers* earned an average of $34,760, only $10 below the national average for that occupation. Considering the magnitude of the gap between an industry wage and the national average provides an indication of the highest paying industries for particular occupations. For each occupation,

---

15 - Even though seniority systems are often found in unionized workplaces, such systems are also a feature of civil service (state and federal governments) and for production workers in manufacturing industries.

the highest-paying industry groups are highlighted in green. All of the industry-occupational wages highlighted in green are at least 10% above the national average for all workers employed in that occupation.

Table 6. Average Annual Earnings of Printing Occupations by Industry Group, 2005

Industry Group	Occupational Title					
	Graphic Designer	Desktop Publisher	Prepress Technician	Press Operator	Job Printer	Bindery Worker
PRINT	$37,810	$36,770	$34,820	$33,550	$33,270	$27,160
Publish	$36,961	$32,252	$33,558	$36,273	$35,914	$26,636
Adv & Design	$45,743	$36,649	$35,439	$28,076	$28,726	$26,380
Mgmt / Biz Support	$44,958	$37,292	$31,025	$28,113	$31,098	$22,853
Package	$44,145	N/A	$34,799	$33,215	$30,390	$23,370
W&R Trade	$40,260	$29,617	$33,383	$26,389	$34,528	$23,627
Other Mfg	$38,748	$38,454	$32,280	$27,411	$30,982	$27,797
R&D / Other Prof	$48,430	$39,657	$26,532	$32,975	$32,748	$24,930
Educ & Health	$41,076	$34,441	$34,230	$31,857	$33,282	$26,676
Apparel / Textiles	$38,903	N/A	$28,630	$23,528	$18,440	N/A
Other Serv	$45,152	$31,594	$34,092	$32,598	$34,493	$42,253
Govnt	$42,954	$33,660	$45,092	$44,020	$36,680	$41,990
FIRE	$46,614	$34,760	$35,930	$33,310	$37,260	$28,910
Telecom	$44,147	$39,620	$36,500	$41,120	N/A	N/A
NEC*	$41,416	N/A	N/A	N/A	N/A	N/A
National Average	$42,530	$34,770	$34,380	$32,470	$33,320	$26,880

* Graphic Designer is the only occupation with both employment and wage data for the NEC industries.

Note: When an industry group's average earnings for an occupation exceed the All Industries' average, the amount is shown in red. Occupational wage is shown in green when the industry average is greater than or equal to 10% above the national average.

With the exception of **Educ & Health**, **Apparel/Textiles**, and **NEC**, all other industry groups had at least one occupation with above average-earnings. In **Educ & Health**, the differences between the industry group's average and the national average was small for *Job Printers* (–$38), *Prepress Technicians* (–$150), and *Bindery Workers* (–$204), and somewhat greater for *Press Operators* (–$613), and *Graphic Designers* (–$1,454). [16] By contrast, in **Apparel/Textiles**, the wages paid to *Job Printers, Press Operators* and *Prepress Technicians* were substantially below the national average, – 44.7% (–$14,880), –27.5% (–$8,942), and –16.7% (–$5,750), respectively. [17] The gap between **Apparel/Textiles'** wages and the all-industries average was smallest for *Graphic Designers*, who earned –$3,628 less, a difference of –8.5% from the all-industries average for this occupation.[18]

Telecom is the only industry group in which the average wage of workers in each core occupation was higher than the national average. Moreover, for two occupations, in particular, **Telecom** paid well above the average. Compared to other industry groups, **Telecom** paid the highest wages to *Desktop Publishers* (virtually tied with **R&D/Other Prof**), with workers earning 14% more than the typical *Desktop Publisher*. *Press Operators* also earned substantially higher wages in **Telecom** ($8,650 more than the all-industries average). Only **Govnt** paid higher average wages to *Press Operators* ($11,550 more than the national average).

For the *Graphic Designer*, the highest wages were paid to workers in **R&D/Other Prof** and **FIRE**. On average, *Graphic Designers'* earnings were $5,900 higher in **R&D/Other Prof** and $4,084 above the all-industries average in **FIRE**. As noted above, **R&D/Other Prof** also paid the highest wages (virtually the same as **Telecom**) for *Desktop Publishers*. In **Other Mfg** (second highest after **R&D/Other Prof** and **Telecom**), *Desktop Publishers* earned $38,454, 10.6% above the all-industries average for this occupation. By a substantial margin, *Prepress Technicians* in **Govnt** were the highest paid, earning $10,712 more (31.2% more) than the national average. *Prepress Technicians* in **Telecom** and **FIRE** were the second and third highest paid workers, with average earnings that exceeded the national average by 6.2% and 4.5%, respectively.

For *Production Printers*, **Govnt, Telecom, Publish**, and **FIRE** paid the highest wages. *Press Operators* employed by **Govnt** earned $11,550 more than the average worker did. **Telecom** and **Publish** were the second and third highest paying industry groups for *Press Operators*, with average earnings exceeding the national average by $8,650 and $3,803, respectively. **FIRE** paid the highest wages to *Job Printers* ($37,260, 11.8% higher than all industries' average), exceeding the average wages paid by **Govnt** ($36,680) by only $580. With the third highest wages in **Publish**, *Job Printers* earned $35,914 (7.8% higher than all industries' average).[19] Five industry groups paid higher wages to *Bindery Workers* than the average paid to all workers employed in that occupation. However, the two highest paying groups—**Other Serv** and **Govnt**—paid an average of $15,373 and $15,110 *more* than the national average.

16 - For *Graphic Designers*, **Educ & Health** paid, on average, –3.4% less. For *Press Operators*, the difference was –1.9% less than the national average. In the construction and utilities industries (**NEC**), *Graphic Designers* earned –$1,114 less, a difference of only –2.6%.

17 - Only **R&D/Other Prof** paid lower wages for *Prepress Technicians*, –$7,848 less than the all-industries average, (a difference of –22.8%).

18 - Three other industry groups had lower wages than **Apparel/Textiles** for the *Graphic Designer* occupation. In **Other Mfg, PRINT**, and **Publish**, the average wages of *Graphic Designers* were, respectively, –8.9%, –11.1%, and –13.1% less than the all-industries average.

19 - Note that **Telecom** did not employ any *Job Printers* in 2005.

Within the same occupation, earnings distributions tend to be skewed, with a few workers earning very high wages. As a result, the majority of workers will earn less than the average – the median is less than the mean. For each core printing occupation, Table 7 shows the average annual earnings, the median, and the wages at the 75th and 90th percentiles of the earnings distribution. For all core printing occupations, 50% or more of the workforce earned less than the national average for that occupation. Moreover, for all core printing occupations, 10% of the workforce (the 90th percentile) had wages that were at least 50% higher than the median wage. The greatest difference in earnings between the top 10th percentile and the median occurred in the *Graphic Designer* occupation, where the 90th percentile wage was nearly 75% higher than the median.

The 75th percentile wage represents the threshold wage for the top 25% of the workforce in an occupation. As such, it may serve as an indicator of the extent of high-wage employment in an industry group for a particular occupation. The next section assesses the extent of high-wage (and low-wage) employment opportunities in each industry group for all core printing occupations.

An industry group may employ only a few workers at very high wages while others in the same occupation are employed at relatively low wages. Under such circumstances, it is possible for an industry group's average wage to be higher than the all-industries average wage for that occupation. The extent to which occupational employment within an industry group is "high-wage" can be computed in reference to the national distribution of earnings for that occupation. In addition to the average, industry wage data from the OES included information on the level of wages for the 10th, 25th, 50th (median), 75th, and 90th percentiles. Using the 75th percentile wage as a

Table 7. Distribution of Earnings in 2005 for Core Printing Occupations — Median, 75th and 90th Percentiles

Earning Characteristics	Occupational Title					
	Graphic Designer	Desktop Publisher	Prepress Technician	Press Operator	Job Printer	Bindery Worker
Average Earnings, All Industries	$42,530	$34,770	$34,380	$32,470	$33,320	$26,880
Median (50th Percentile)	$38,390	$32,800	$32,840	$30,730	$31,920	$25,050
75th Percentile	$51,360	$43,000	$42,350	$40,230	$40,430	$32,760
90th Percentile	$67,660	$53,750	$52,800	$49,870	$50,110	$41,470
Percent Difference 90th to Median*	76.2%	63.9%	60.8%	62.3%	57.0%	65.5%

* Percent Difference in Earnings = (90th − 50th percentile) ÷ 50th percentile earnings × 100

benchmark to assess the extent of high-wage employment for each core printing occupation and the four percentile wages available for each industry, a count of high-wage jobs was constructed for all core printing occupations. Similarly, low-wage jobs in an industry are identified as all those that are less than or equal to the 25th percentile wage for all workers in a particular occupation.

In each industry with any occupational employment, the earnings distribution for that occupation is divided into five cumulative frequency intervals — 10th percentile (e.g., 90% of the industry's workforce employed in the occupation have higher wages), 25th percentile, the median (50th percentile), 75th percentile, and the 90th percentile. Because industry employment distributions are grouped in such large intervals, in some cases the interval data would be only a few hundred dollars (or less) different from the all-industries' 25th and 75th percentile wages. Rounding the percentile wage to the nearest $1,000 allows a closer approximation of high and low wage jobs in each industry group. For each occupation in Tables 8 and 11, the all-industries' 25th and 75th percentile earnings are included along with the threshold (nearest $1,000) level used to compute high and low wages jobs in all industry groups.

Design & Prepress Occupations

Table 8 shows the industry distribution of occupational employment in high- and low-wage jobs. The industry groups with the most employment in all *Design & Prepress* occupations are listed at the top, while those industry groups with the fewest jobs are shown at the bottom. For each occupation, both high- and low-wage status were calibrated to the earnings distribution for that occupation. Starting with the 75th percentile wage for *Graphic Designer*, the high-wage threshold for *Graphic Designers* was $51,000; for the *Prepress Technician*, all jobs that paid greater than or equal to $42,000 were considered to be high-wage. The low-wage thresholds for the *Desktop Publisher* and *Prepress Technician* were the same, below $25,000. For the *Graphic Designer* the low-wage threshold was $30,000.

Only two industry groups — **FIRE** and **Educ & Health** — had a greater percentage of high-wage jobs than the percentage of low-wage jobs for all three *Design & Prepress* occupations. In two other industry groups, there was *no* occupation where the number of low-wage jobs exceeded the number of high-wage job. **Telecom** had a higher percentage of high-wage jobs in the *Graphic Designer* and *Desktop Publisher* occupations and the same percentage (25%) of high and low-wage jobs for the *Prepress Technician*. **Package** did not employ any *Desktop Publishers*. However, like **Telecom**, there were a higher percentage of high-wage to low-wage *Graphic Designers* and the same percentage (10%) of high- and low-wage *Prepress Technicians*.

In **Educ & Health**, workers earned less than the all-industry average in each *Design & Prepress* occupation, although the differences were small. With respect to differences in the proportion of high- and low-wage jobs, the differences are also small. For every 10 high-wage jobs for *Graphic Designers* and *Prepress Technicians*, there were 9 low-wage jobs in **Educ & Health**. For *Desktop Publishers*, the difference was even smaller — for every 100 workers employed in high-wage jobs, 98 would be employed at low-wages. By contrast, in **FIRE**, there was a substantial difference in the shares of high- and low-wage jobs among *Graphic Designers* — 4 high-wage jobs for every low-wage job. For both *Desktop Publishers* and *Prepress Technicians*, there were 2-3 high-wage jobs per low-wage job.

Table 8. High- and Low-Wage Share of Industry Group's Employment in Design & Prepress Occupations

Industry Group	Graphic Designer		Desktop Publisher		Prepress Technician	
	High-Wage	Low-Wage	High-Wage	Low-Wage	High-Wage	Low-Wage
PRINT	10.0%	25.0%	25.0%	10.0%	25.0%	10.0%
Publish	10.1%	24.9%	10.0%	24.9%	25.0%	25.0%
Adv& Design	25.0%	17.3%	14.7%	20.3%	25.0%	18.8%
R&D / Other Prof	24.4%	11.3%	27.1%	8.6%	12.7%	44.5%
W&R Trade	14.6%	20.2%	14.3%	19.5%	16.1%	14.5%
Mgmt / Biz Support	23.6%	13.1%	21.3%	15.8%	12.1%	28.5%
Other Mfg	15.5%	19.0%	27.1%	9.1%	9.7%	16.3%
Educ & Health	13.2%	12.2%	10.8%	10.6%	12.8%	12.0%
Other Serv	19.0%	13.9%	11.8%	22.2%	16.5%	19.5%
Package	22.8%	12.2%	N/A	N/A	10.0%	10.0%
FIRE	26.0%	6.5%	27.2%	10.1%	25.0%	10.0%
Govnt	19.1%	10.0%	10.0%	20.9%	48.3%	10.3%
Telecom	27.0%	25.7%	25.0%	10.0%	25.0%	25.0%
Apparel / Textiles	11.6%	24.6%	N/A	N/A	0.0%	25.0%
NEC	14.3%	18.4%	N/A	N/A	N/A	N/A
Threshold Wage*	$51,000	$30,000	$43,000	$25,000	$42,000	$25,000
Percentile Wage[†]	$51,360	$29,460	$43,000	$24,950	$42,350	$24,880

*For high-wage jobs, the minimum threshold wage is the 75th percentile rounded down to the next $1,000. For low-wage jobs, the maximum threshold wage is the 25th percentile rounded up to the next $1,000.

[†]High-wage is the 75th percentile and low-wage is the 25th percentile of all workers employed in the occupation in 2005.

In **Telecom**, the difference in high- and low-wage shares was greatest for *Desktop Publishers*, with 2-3 high-wage jobs per low-wage job. In **Package**, this difference was greatest among *Graphic Designers*, with approximately 2 high-wage jobs for every low-wage job.

The industry group that paid the highest wages to *Desktop Publishers* and *Prepress Technicians* also employed substantially more high-wage than low-wage jobs in these occupations. With the highest average wage for *Desktop Publishers*, **R&D/Other Prof** employed 3.2 workers earning more than $43,000 for every *Desktop Publisher* who earned less than $25,000 (low-wage threshold). In comparison to any other group, **Govnt** paid the highest wages for *Prepress Technicians*. Additionally, for every *Prepress Technician* who earned less than $25,000, there were 4-5 workers who earned more than $42,000 per year.

At the other extreme, two industry groups — **Apparel/Textiles** and **NEC** — had more low-wage than high-wage jobs in each *Design & Prepress* occupation with any employment. Only *Graphic Designers* and *Prepress Technicians* were employed in **Apparel/Textiles**, and *Graphic Designers* were the only occupation with any employment in the construction and utilities industries (**NEC**).[20] Although no industry group had a greater proportion of low-wage jobs for all three occupations, **Publish** had more low-wage than high-wage jobs for *Graphic Designers* and *Desktop Publishers*, with the same proportion of high- and low-wage jobs for *Prepress Technicians* (25%). Hence, **Publish** is the only other industry group in which there was no *Design & Prepress* occupation that had more high-wage than low-wage jobs.

While 11.2% of *Graphic Designers* earned more than $51,000 in **Apparel/Textiles**, there were still two *Graphic Designers* earning less than $30,000 for every high-wage *Graphic Designer* employed in this group. In addition, **Apparel/Textiles** was the only industry group where there were no *Prepress Technicians* with earnings above the 75th percentile. Moreover, one out of ever four workers employed in this group earned less than $25,000. In **Publish**, there were 10 low-wage jobs for *Graphic Designers* and *Desktop Publishers* for every 4 high-wage jobs in these occupations (a ratio of 2.5:1). **R&D/Other Prof** had the highest proportion of low-wage to high-wage jobs in a *Design & Prepress* occupation than any other industry group. While *Graphic Designers* and *Desktop Publishers* earned substantially higher wages (on average), there were 7 *Prepress Technicians* who earned less than $25,000 for any 2 workers earning $42,000 or more per year.

Table 9 shows the contribution of each industry group to all *high-wage* jobs and the industry group's share of occupational employment for each *Design & Prepress* occupation. In this table, industry groups are ordered by the number of high-wage jobs in *Design & Prepress* occupations. Table 10 has the same structure as Table 9, but displays each industry group's contribution to *low-wage* jobs relative to its share of employment for each occupation. While the **PRINT** industry contributed the greatest number of high-wage *Design & Prepress* jobs, **Publish** had the most low-wage jobs of any industry group. The same three industries had the most high- and low-wage jobs in the *Design & Prepress* occupations: **PRINT**, **Publish**, and **Adv & Design**. Together, these industry groups employed 62.6% of all workers in *Design & Prepress* occupations, and were responsible for 64% of all high-wage and 66.7% of all low-wage jobs in these occupations.

20 - In NEC, there were 4 low-wage jobs for every 3 high-wage jobs for Graphic Designers.

Table 9. Contributions by Industry Group to High-Wage Employment in Design & Prepress Occupations, 2005

Industry Group	Graphic Designer		Desktop Publisher		Prepress Technician		Design & Prepress
	High-Wage	All Jobs	High-Wage	All Jobs	High-Wage	All Jobs	High-Wage Jobs
PRINT	5.9%	10.9%	36.4%	25.1%	62.7%	58.9%	14,414
Adv & Design	36.4%	27.0%	6.5%	7.7%	3.3%	3.1%	12,953
Publish	7.8%	14.3%	20.4%	35.1%	25.6%	24.1%	7,960
R&D / Other Prof	12.8%	9.8%	7.3%	5.4%	0.5%	1.0%	4,710
Mgmt / Biz Support	9.6%	7.6%	10.1%	8.2%	1.3%	2.5%	3,917
W&R Trade	7.1%	9.0%	2.5%	3.0%	0.8%	1.2%	2,628
Other Mfg	5.1%	6.1%	3.1%	2.0%	1.1%	2.0%	2,028
Other Serv	4.0%	3.9%	2.7%	3.9%	0.3%	0.4%	1,504
FIRE	2.4%	1.7%	7.9%	5.0%	0.3%	0.3%	1,243
Educ & Health	2.8%	4.0%	2.1%	3.4%	0.5%	0.8%	1,119
Package	1.5%	1.3%	0.0%	0.0%	2.0%	4.8%	855
Telecom	2.3%	1.6%	0.2%	0.1%	0.02%	0.01%	791
Govnt	1.2%	1.2%	0.7%	1.2%	1.7%	0.8%	729
Apparel / Textiles	0.9%	1.4%	N/A	N/A	0.0%	0.1%	298
NEC	0.2%	0.3%	N/A	N/A	N/A	N/A	82
Employment Totals	33,199	178,490	5,125	29,790	16,907	71,950	55,231
Percent of Design & Prepress Total*	60.1%	63.7%	9.3%	10.6%	30.6%	25.7%	19.7%[†]

*For each occupation, high-wage percent refers to the occupation's share of all high-wage Design & Prepress jobs (55,231), whereas the all jobs percent refers to the occupation's share of total employment in the three Design & Prepress occupations (280,230).

[†]All high-wage jobs as percent of total employment in Design & Prepress occupations.

Table 10. Contributions by Industry Group to Low-Wage Employment in Design & Prepress Occupations, 2005

Industry Group	Graphic Designer		Desktop Publisher		Prepress Technician		Design & Prepress
	Low-Wage	All Jobs	Low-Wage	All Jobs	Low-Wage	All Jobs	Low-Wage Jobs
Publish	19.4%	14.3%	50.4%	35.1%	40.4%	24.1%	13,271
PRINT	14.9%	10.9%	14.5%	25.1%	39.4%	58.9%	9,856
Adv & Design	25.6%	27.0%	9.0%	7.7%	3.8%	3.1%	9,226
W&R Trade	10.0%	9.0%	3.4%	3.0%	1.2%	1.2%	3,570
Mgmt / Biz Support	5.4%	7.6%	7.5%	8.2%	4.7%	2.5%	2,663
R&D / Other Prof	6.0%	9.8%	2.7%	5.4%	2.9%	1.0%	2,411
Other Mfg	6.3%	6.1%	1.0%	2.0%	2.2%	2.0%	2,357
Other Serv	2.9%	3.9%	5.0%	3.9%	0.5%	0.4%	1,274
Educ & Health	2.7%	4.0%	2.1%	3.4%	0.7%	0.8%	1,044
Telecom	2.2%	1.6%	0.1%	0.1%	0.03%	0.01%	737
Apparel / Textiles	1.9%	1.4%	N/A	N/A	0.2%	0.1%	650
Package	0.8%	1.3%	N/A	N/A	3.2%	4.8%	618
FIRE	0.6%	1.7%	2.9%	5.0%	0.2%	0.3%	366
Govnt	0.7%	1.2%	1.5%	1.2%	0.6%	0.8%	353
NEC	0.3%	0.3%	N/A	N/A	N/A	N/A	105
Employment Totals	32,577	178,490	5,167	29,790	10,757	71,950	48,501
Share of Design & Prepress Total *	67.2%	63.7%	10.7%	10.6%	22.2%	25.7%	17.3%[†]

*For each occupation, low-wage percent refers to the occupation's share of all low-wage Design & Prepress jobs (48,501), whereas the all jobs percent refers to the occupation's share of total employment in the three Design & Prepress occupations (280,230).

[†]Percent of all Design & Prepress occupational employment that is low-wage.

A comparison of the totals in Tables 9 and 10 reveal that there were only 622 more jobs that were high-wage than were low-wage for the *Graphic Designer* (33,199 versus 32,577). Although there were more low-wage than high-wage jobs for the *Desktop Publisher* (5,167 versus 5,125), the *Prepress Technician* had high-wage jobs outnumbering low-wage jobs by 6,150 (16,907 versus 10,757). The main explanation for these differences has to do with the wage policies of the industries that employ a substantial share of the workers in these occupations.

The industries that were the largest employers of **Design & Prepress** occupations also employed a substantial share of high-wage workers in these occupations. However, there were substantial differences among these industry groups in the mix of occupations that had high- or low-wage status. In **Adv & Design**, 93.2% of the high-wage jobs were held by *Graphic Designers*. When combined with the two other industry clusters that constitute the **Prof & Biz** industry group, *Graphic Designers* held 90.4% of the high-wage jobs. *Graphic Designers* also accounted for 84.5% of all low-wage jobs in the **Prof & Biz** group. For **PRINT**, 73.5% of high-wage jobs in **Design & Prepress** occupations were held by *Prepress Technicians*. For **Publish**, *Prepress Technicians* were responsible for 54.4% of high-wage employment.

The **PRINT** and **Publish** industry groups had the highest number of high-wage jobs for *Prepress Technicians*. Together, these two industry groups provided 88.3% of the high-wage jobs for that occupation in 2005. Both industry groups contributed approximately the same number of low-wage jobs in the *Prepress Technician* occupation (4,345 in **Publish** and 4,239 in *PRINT*). With the exceptions of **PRINT** and **Publish**, the *Graphic Designer* constituted the vast majority of high-wage jobs in other industry groups, contributing 60.1% of all high-wage jobs in the **Design & Prepress** occupations. Moreover, the *Graphic Designer* dominated low-wage jobs in the **Design & Prepress** occupations in all other industry groups.

Production Printers and Bindery Workers

The **PRINT** industry employed 55.9% of all *Production Printers* and 77.1% of all *Bindery Workers* in 2005. Still, over 100,000 *Production Printers* and more than 14,000 *Bindery Workers* were employed in other industries. Moreover, employment of *Production Printers* in other industries is expected to increase over the next ten years. Industry differences in wages can be important in attracting new workers and increasing (or decreasing) the mobility of skilled workers between industries. Table 11 shows the relative importance of high-wage and low-wage jobs in each industry group for the occupations of *Press Operator*, *Job Printer*, and *Bindery Worker*. Industry groups are shown in rank order, from the largest to smallest employers of production printers.

Among the industry groups in which the high-wage share of jobs for **Production Printers** or *Bindery Workers* constituted 25% (or more) of the jobs, there were five groups that also had the same (or higher percentage) of high-wage jobs in at least one **Design & Prepress** occupation: **PRINT**, **FIRE**, **Telecom**, **Publish**, and **Govnt**. However, **Govnt** stands out as the only employer in which the majority of the jobs in a specific occupation were high-wage. Sixty-five percent of all *Bindery Workers* employed by **Govnt** in 2005 were paid more than $32,000, which was the 75th percentile threshold wage for that occupation at that time. Moreover, 34.5% of all *Press Operators* employed by **Govnt** earned above $40,000. For *Job Printers*, **FIRE** and **Other Serv** had a greater proportion of high-wage jobs than all other groups, 29.2% and 30.9%, respectively. **PRINT** was the only industry group in which

Table 11. High- and Low-Wage Share of Industry Group's Employment in Production Printer and Bindery Worker Occupations

Industry Group	Press Operator		Job Printer		Bindery Worker	
	High-Wage	Low-Wage	High-Wage	Low-Wage	High-Wage	Low-Wage
PRINT	25.0%	10.0%	25.0%	10.0%	25.0%	10.0%
Publish	25.0%	10.0%	25.0%	25.0%	10.0%	25.0%
Package	20.8%	14.2%	10.0%	25.1%	10.0%	25.0%
Adv & Design	10.0%	25.0%	10.0%	46.1%	16.4%	18.6%
Other Mfg	9.8%	29.7%	16.7%	19.4%	20.8%	8.8%
W&R Trade	5.8%	36.2%	6.8%	25.0%	11.5%	22.5%
Mgmt / Biz Support	8.7%	25.0%	11.7%	24.8%	10.1%	46.7%
Apparel / Textiles	1.7%	50.0%	0.0%	75.0%	N/A	N/A
Educ & Health	11.4%	14.6%	17.0%	14.0%	18.5%	14.5%
Govnt	34.5%	6.8%	25.0%	10.0%	65.1%	3.3%
Other Serv	15.4%	21.1%	30.9%	15.9%	24.2%	10.0%
R&D / Other Prof	17.8%	19.5%	16.3%	18.5%	16.0%	40.0%
FIRE	14.6%	19.6%	29.2%	8.4%	25.3%	10.0%
Telecom	25.0%	10.0%	N/A	N/A	N/A	N/A
Threshold Wage*	$40,000	$24,000	$40,000	$25,000	$32,000	$20,000
Percentile Wage[†]	$40,230	$23,050	$40,430	$24,790	$32,760	$19,680

* For high-wage jobs, the minimum threshold wage is the 75th percentile rounded down to the next $1,000. For low-wage jobs, the maximum threshold wage is the 25th percentile rounded up to the next $1,000.

[†] High-wage is the 75th percentile and low-wage is the 25th percentile of all workers employed in the occupation in 2005.

the high-wage proportion of jobs was 25% for both types of *Production Printer* occupations and for the *Bindery Worker* occupation. Along with **PRINT**, **Publish** and **Govnt** were the only other industry groups in which 25% of the jobs were high-wage for both the *Press Operator* and *Job Printer*.

Only two industry groups — **PRINT** and **Govnt** — had a greater percentage of high-wage jobs than the percentage of low-wage jobs for all three occupations. As for dominance of low-wage jobs, four industry groups — **Adv & Design**, **Mgmt/Biz Support**, **W&R Trade**, and **R&D/Other Prof** — had a greater percentage of low-wage jobs than high-wage jobs for both types of *Production Printer* and for the *Bindery Worker* occupation as well. Moreover, since no *Bindery Workers* were employed in **Apparel/Textiles**, this industry group also had a greater percentage of low-wage jobs than high-wage jobs for *Press Operators* and *Job Printers*. Moreover, 75% of all *Job Printers* employed in **Apparel/Textiles** earned less than $25,000 (the low-wage threshold) and no *Job Printer* had earnings above the 75th percentile.

The vast majority of high-wage *Bindery Workers* (86.3%) were employed in the **PRINT** industry. However, one-third (33.7%) of high-wage and 63.6% of low-wage jobs for *Production Printers* were in industries other than **PRINT**. Only 1,968 high-wage *Bindery Workers* were employed in all other industries. The **PRINT** industry alone was responsible for 55.1% of all low-wage bindery jobs. Together, **PRINT**, **Publish**, and **Mgmt/Biz Support** had 88.7% of all low-wage jobs for *Bindery Workers*. For these reasons, the contributions of other industries to high- and low-wage bindery jobs were not analyzed in the same detail as the *Production Printer* occupations. Thus, Table 12 shows only the industry contributions to high- and low-wage employment for the occupations of *Press Operator* and *Job Printer*. Table 12 shows that there were 37.5% more high-wage than low-wage jobs, whereas, for *Design & Prepress* occupations, high-wage jobs outnumbered low-wage jobs by only 13.9%

As in Table 11, industry groups are arrayed by their overall employment of *Production Printers*, with the industry groups at the top having the most jobs and those at the bottom employing the fewest workers in these occupations. In all, there were 51,203 high-wage and 37,246 low-wage jobs for *Production Printers* identified with specific industries. The *Press Operator* and *Job Printer* shares of *Production Printer* occupational employment were 79.2% and 20.8% respectively. The proportionate shares of low-wage jobs were similar to the relative employment shares of the two printer occupations, although there were more high-wage *Job Printers* (22.6%) relative to the occupation's share of employment. With the exception of **Apparel/Textiles** (and **Telecom** with no employment), all other industry groups contributed to both low-wage and high-wage employment of *Job Printers*. Relative to their shares of employment in both occupations, **PRINT** and **Govnt** were the only industry groups that contributed a greater proportion of high-wage and a smaller proportion of low-wage jobs for the *Press Operator* and the *Job Printer*.

With respect to *Press Operators*, four industry groups contributed a disproportionate share of high-wage jobs, while five industry groups contributed disproportionately to low-wage employment. **PRINT**, **Publish**, **Package**, and **Govnt** are the only industry groups that contributed a higher proportion of high-wage jobs and a lower proportion of low-wage jobs for *Press Operators* than would be expected considering their contributions to occupational employment in 2005. The contributions of **PRINT**, **Publish**, **Package**, and **Govnt** to *Press Operator's*

Table 12. Industry Contribution to All High- and Low-Wage Jobs for Press Operators and Job Printers, 2005

| Industry Group* | Industry Contributions to Occupational Employment (%) | | | | | | Industry Employment of Production Printers | |
| | Press Operator | | | Job Printer | | | | |
	High-Wage	Low-Wage	All Jobs	High-Wage	Low-Wage	All Jobs	High-Wage	Low-Wage
PRINT	64.4%	34.5%	53.1%	72.4%	44.1%	66.5%	33,923	13,569
Publish	12.43	6.6%	10.2%	16.4%	25.0%	15.1%	6,785	3,860
Package	10.9%	10.0%	10.8%	0.5%	1.7%	1.0%	4,383	3,088
Adv & Design	2.6%	8.7%	5.4%	1.6%	11.2%	3.7%	1,221	3,443
Other Mfg	2.6%	10.4%	5.4%	1.4%	2.4%	1.9%	1,173	3,260
Govnt	2.4%	0.6%	1.4%	0.8%	0.5%	0.7%	1,031	222
Educ & Health	1.1%	1.9%	2.0%	2.6%	3.2%	3.4%	745	817
Mgmt / Biz Support	1.3%	5.1%	3.1%	1.9%	6.0%	3.6%	737	1,966
W&R Trade	1.1%	8.9%	3.8%	0.7%	3.7%	2.2%	498	2,928
Other Serv	0.3%	0.6%	0.4%	0.9%	0.7%	0.6%	222	220
R&D / Other Prof	0.4%	0.5%	0.4%	0.4%	0.7%	0.5%	186	205
FIRE	0.3%	0.5%	0.4%	0.6%	0.3%	0.5%	174	156
Apparel / Textiles	0.3%	11.7%	3.6%	0.0%	0.6%	0.1%	120	3,510
Telecom	0.01%	0.01%	0.01%	N/A	N/A	N/A	5	2
Total	39,607	29,629	192,410	11,596	7,617	50,510	51,203	37,246
Share of Total Printers**	77.4%	79.5%	79.2%	22.6%	20.5%	20.8%	21.1%[†]	15.3%[†]

* Industry groups are listed in rank order by employment of high-wage Production Printers.

** Total refers to employment in the occupation for each category—high-wage, low-wage, all jobs.

[†]For high- and low-wage Production Printers, "total" refers to all employment of Production Printers in these industries.

occupational employment were 53.1%, 10.2%, 10.8%, and 1.4% respectively. Of all industry-identified high-wage jobs for this occupation, **PRINT**, **Publish**, **Package**, and **Govnt** accounted for 64.4%, 12.3%, 10.9%, and 2.4%, respectively. In all, these four industry groups were responsible for 90.0% of all high-wage jobs for the *Press Operator* occupation. Moreover, these industry groups' contributions to low-wage jobs were substantially less than their shares of occupational employment.

While the **PRINT** industry was the single largest contributor to low–wage jobs for *Production Printers*, other industries were responsible for the majority of low-wage employment of *Press Operators* (65.5%) and of *Job Printers* (55.9%). In addition to the industries identified in the previous paragraph, **Educ & Health** was the only other industry with a relatively smaller contribution to low-wage jobs than its share of all jobs for *Press Operators*.[21] Eight industry groups had a greater share of low-wage jobs than expected in comparison to their shares of occupational employment for the *Press Operator*. The industry groups that contributed the most low-wage jobs were **Apparel/Textiles** (11.7%), **Other Mfg** (10.4%), **W&R Trade** (8.9%), **Adv & Design** (8.7%), and **Mgmt/Biz Support** (5.1%). Together, these five industry groups were responsible for 44.8% of low-wage jobs (13,290 *Press Operators*) – more than double their combined total share of occupational employment (21.3%).

For the *Job Printer*, nine industry groups had disproportionate shares of low-wage employment relative to their contributions to all industry-assigned employment. Together, these industry groups were responsible for 3,956 low-wage jobs (52% of the total), while contributing only 28.7% of employment. Of these, the largest contributors to low-wage employment for the *Job Printer* were **Publish** (25.0%), **Adv & Design** (11.2%) and **Mgmt/Biz Support** (6.0%).

---

21 - **Telecom** had the same shares of all jobs and of low-wage jobs for this occupation.

SECTION V: OCCUPATIONAL EMPLOYMENT CHANGES FROM 2001 TO 2005

At each stage of the printing process — *Design & Prepress*, *Print Production*, and *Postpress/Bindery* — computers, electronic controls, imaging devices, and a number of other technological changes are expected to affect the growth in employment. According to the U.S. Bureau of Labor Statistics, the demand for *Graphic Designers* who are adept at using computers to plan and create their designs is expected to increase over the next decade, as is the demand for *Desktop Publishers*. As electronic prepress technologies become more widely used, there will be fewer jobs in such traditional prepress technical specialties as paste-up, photography and film processing, and plate making in the era of electronic prepress.

In *Print Production*, the demand for *Job Printers* — a hybrid occupation that requires a combination of skills in layout, prepress, and press operating tasks — is expected to increase. While the demand for *Press Operators* is also expected to grow, productivity improvements in press technology is expected to result in a slower rate of job growth in comparison to the growth of *Job Printers*. The demand for the *Job Printer* is expected to grow at a faster rate because prepress, press operation, and some postpress tasks are combined in this occupation. Employment growth for the *Job Printer* is likely to be associated with the growth of "quick" printing. Quick printing includes all the small-scale storefront printing establishments that do "short-run offset printing or prepress services, in combination with providing document photocopying service[s]". [22] To the extent that printing activities in other industries resemble "quick" printing, and based on the fact that these operations have expanded since 2001, we would expect to see relatively more growth in the employment of *Job Printers* relative to *Press Operators* outside the **PRINT** industry. As for *Bindery Workers*, increased mechanization of the tasks now performed with hand tools will reduce employment in this occupation.[23]

The questions addressed in this section include:

➢ At the national level, which occupations have shown increases (decreases) in employment?

➢ Which industry groups have increased (decreased) employment for occupations that show an overall job loss (gain) at the national level?

➢ How much employment growth has occurred outside the printing industry?

➢ Outside the printing industry, which industries have increased employment in *Design & Prepress* or *Production Printer* occupations?

National Occupational Employment

Occupational Employment Estimates for 2000 and 2001

With only five years of data, the selection of a base year for analyzing employment growth (or decline) is critical. Since the year 2000 represents a peak period for printing industry revenues and employment in some segments of the industry, while 2001 was a recession period, the latter is preferred as a base year for analyzing

22 - Source: U.S. Census Bureau, 1997 NAICS Definitions, 323114 Quick Printing.

23 - Bureau of Labor Statistics, *Occupational Outlook Handbook, 2002-3 Edition*, pp. 75-79.

employment growth in core printing occupations. Another reason for preferring 2001 is the greater industry detail and precision in estimating occupational employment changes within industry groups. The 2001 industry occupational employment estimates are more reliable, as they are based on a sample of establishments that was 50% larger than the sample used to estimate occupational employment in 2000. Moreover, the 2001 data provide both two- and three-digit SIC industry classifications, making it possible to assign occupational employment to an industry at a higher level of aggregation. As a result, there are fewer cases of industries in which employment estimates are missing from estimates of industry group employment. In 2000, there were 21,940 jobs in core printing occupations that could not be assigned to a specific industry. Hence, the 2000 industry occupational employment estimates exclude 3.4% of all jobs in core printing occupations. By contrast, in 2001, only 3,830 jobs could not be identified with a specific industry. [24] Thus, the industry-based occupational employment estimates undercount employment by less than one percent—0.6% to be exact.

For the printing industry in particular, sales revenues peaked in 2000 after a seven-year period of sustained growth from 1994 to 2000. Industry revenues then fell to $100.8 billion in 2001 from $104.4 billion in 2000, a decrease of $3.5 billion (-3.4%). The industry as a whole continued to experience revenue losses in 2002 totaling $5.1 billion (-5.1%). However, much of that loss reflects a decline in certain specializations within the industry. In the new sub-classifications within commercial printing—gravure, screen, quick, and digital—revenues increased by $3.0 billion between 2001 and 2002. Moreover, with reductions in other segments of the printing industry in the same period, the importance of these commercial print specializations to the industry grew from 14.5% in 2001 to 18.3% in 2002. While overall employment in the industry reached its peak in 1998, the printing industry as a whole did not experience substantial job losses until 2001. Overall, the printing industry lost 31,694 jobs between 2000 and 2001, a reduction of 3.8%.[25] Employment reductions continued in 2002, with a loss of 58,900 jobs—10.3% less than industry employment in 2001. Nationally, the OES employment data show that there were 25,910 fewer jobs in core printing occupations in 2001, representing a reduction of 4.0% from 2000. In contrast to the printing industry as a whole, the 2001 to 2002 reduction in core printing occupational employment was smaller, with a total job loss of 22,180 (a decrease of 3.6%). Thus, even though job losses continued to occur in core printing occupations, the greatest job loss occurred in the previous period (2000 – 2001). For analyses of trends in employment growth, it is important to separate the cyclical reductions in employment that is temporary, resulting from a slowdown in the economy from the changes in employment that occur during a period of expansion. As a base year, 2001 is preferable since much of the cyclically related employment reductions have already occurred.

National Patterns of Occupational Employment Growth 2001-2005

Figure 10 shows all employment in each core printing occupation for 2001 and 2005. The occupations are arrayed from the most to the fewest jobs in 2005. In both years, more workers were employed as *Press Operators* than any other occupation, while *Desktop Publishers* had the fewest jobs. While the number of *Press Operators* was

24 - The missing 3,830 jobs represent 0.6% of the national total in all core printing occupations. Out of the 3,830 cases, *Desktop Publishers* accounted for 290 cases, while *Graphic Designers* accounted for 840 cases. See the Technical Appendix for more details on the treatment of missing industry (and industry group) counts.

25 - Sources: *2002 Economic Census and Annual Industry Shipments Series*, Bureau of Economic Affairs, U.S. Department of Commerce.

nearly the same in 2001 and 2005 (198,710 and 192,520 respectively), there was substantial growth in the employment of *Graphic Designers*, with an increase from 136,470 jobs in 2001 to 178,530 in 2005 (a growth of 30.8%).

Figure 11 shows the national occupational employment changes as an overall percentage increase (decrease) from 2001 employment levels, as well as the average annual increase (decrease). The occupations are arranged from right to left by the greatest percentage increase to the greatest percentage decrease in jobs. Thus, employment of *Graphic Designers* increased by 30%, while at the other extreme, *Bindery Workers* had a 31% reduction in jobs between 2001 and 2005. In terms of the number of jobs, the *Press Operator* occupation had greater job loss than the *Job Printer*. When measured as a percentage change in employment, the *Press Operator* shows the smallest reduction of all core printing occupations that sustained reductions during the period, with a job loss of only 3.1% between 2001 and 2005. Comparing the annualized rates of change for 2001 to 2005 to the change from 2000 to 2001, the *Graphic Designer* occupation increased employment at an average annual rate of 7.7% during the later period, in contrast to the modest 2.1% increase between 2000 and 2001. For the *Press Operator*, the annualized rate of job loss was only 0.8%, in contrast to the to 7.5% reduction in *Press Operators* that occurred between 2000 and 2001. With the exception of *Job Printers*, the annualized percent reduction in jobs for 2001 to 2005 was smaller than the reductions that occurred between 2000 and 2001.[26]

Figure 10. Employment in Core Printing Occupations, 2001 and 2005

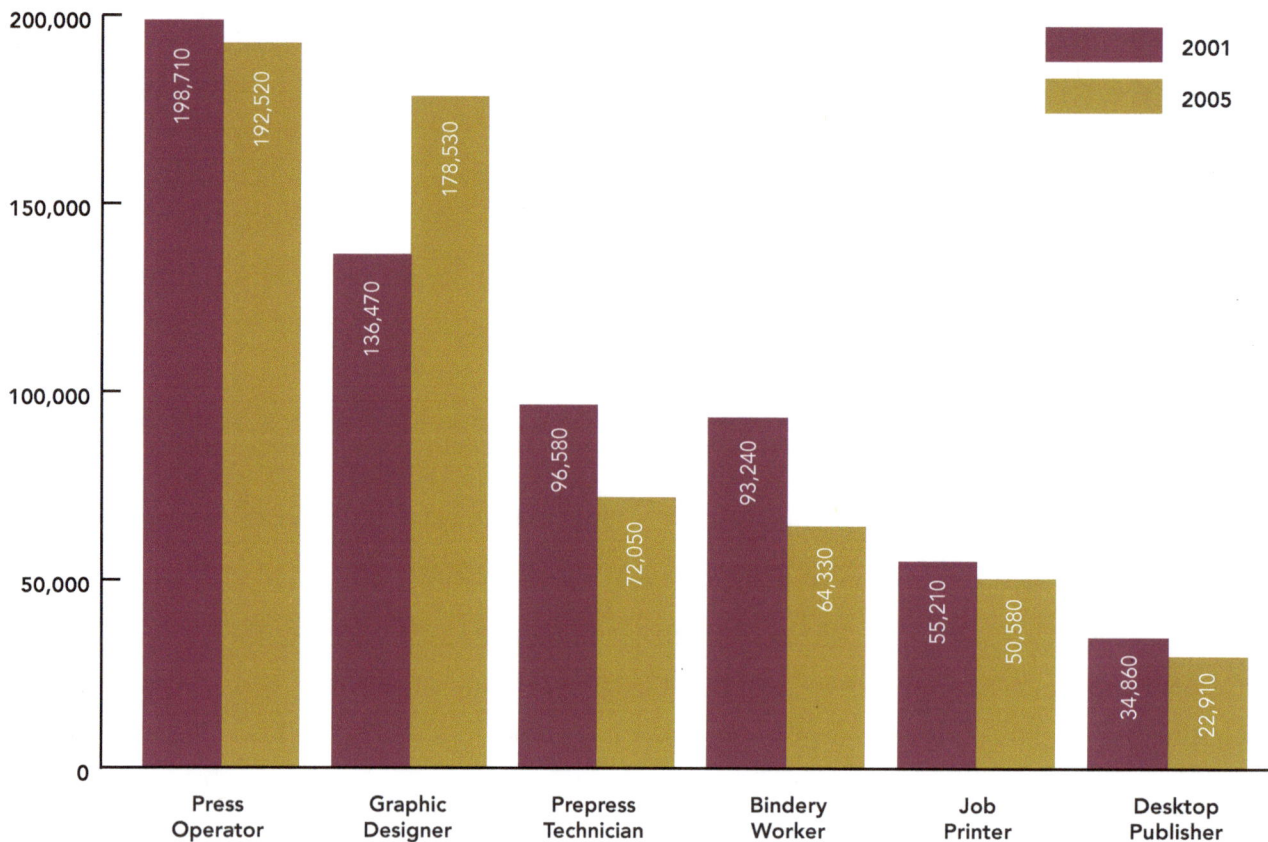

26 - The *Job Printer* was the only occupation with an increase in employment (10.3%) in 2000 to 2001 that was then followed by job losses in later years, with a net reduction of 8.4% from 2001 to 2005.

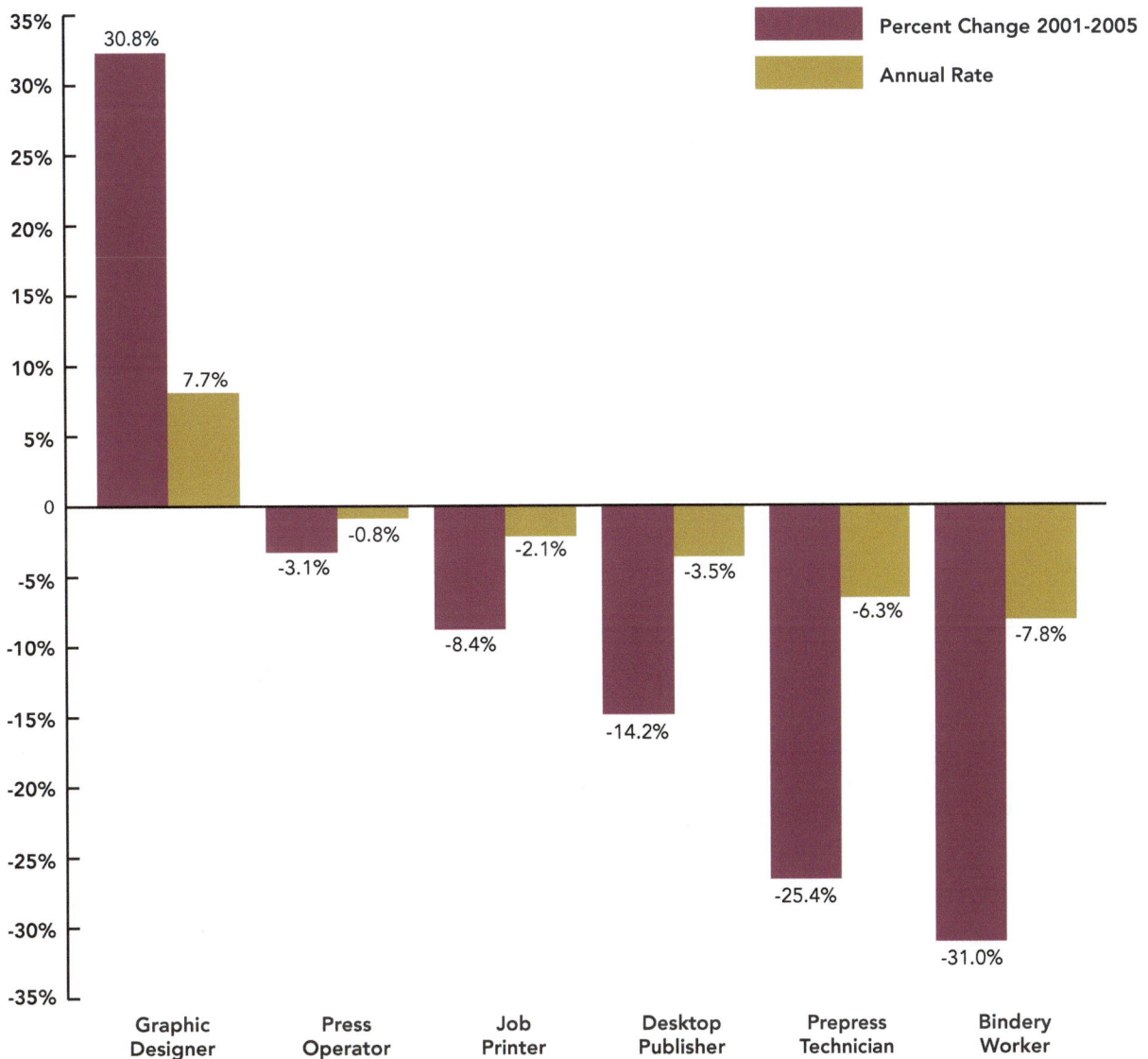

For each printing occupation, Table 13 compares the net employment changes that occurred nationally to the gross increases and decreases in employment that occurred as a result of industry group changes in employment. The gross increase in employment is calculated as the sum of employment increases for industry groups that had any job growth in that occupation. Gross decreases represent the sum of all job losses by industry groups that had reductions in employment for the same occupation. All core printing occupations, including the *Graphic Designer*, had decreases in employment in some industries. Moreover, even for those occupations with substantial job losses nationally, there were some industry groups that increased employment.

Table 13. Employment Changes in Core Printing Occupations, 2001-2005

	Core Printing Occupations						All Core Occupations
	Graphic Designer	Job Printer	Desktop Publisher	Press Operator	Prepress Technician	Bindery Worker	
Net Change, National Employment	42,060	-4,630	-4,950	-6,190	-24,530	-28,910	-27,150
Gross Job Increases	47,950	3,720	4,050	14,540	470	890	71,620
As a % of All Increases	67.0%	5.2%	5.7%	20.3%	0.7%	1.2%	
Gross Job Losses	-5,090	-7,910	-8,830	-20,340	-24,260	-29,000	-95,430
As a % of All Job Losses	5.3%	8.3%	9.3%	21.3%	25.4%	30.4%	

Note: From left to right, occupations are ordered by the largest net increase to the greatest net loss in employment. Gross increases and decreases are computed for industry groups. For each occupation, the sum of industry increases and decreases is not the same as the net employment change for the nation as a whole, since the total number of jobs assigned to a specific industry were less than the national employment estimates in both years.

Overall, the gross increases in core printing occupations resulted in the addition of 71,620 jobs. However, for every job that was created in one industry, there were 1.3 job reductions in other industry groups. As was apparent in Figures 10 and 11, only the *Graphic Designer* occupation had a net increase in employment nationally. Table 13 shows that *Graphic Designers* contributed most of the increases in employment among industry groups, with 67.0% of the gross total. Following the *Graphic Designer*, the occupation with the second largest employment increases by industry group was the *Press Operator* (14,540 new jobs), contributing 20.3% of the gross increase in employment for all core occupations. However, the substantial employment reductions of *Press Operators* by some industries resulted in a net loss of 6,190 jobs for this occupation between 2001 and 2005. For the other four core occupations, there was a gross increase of only 9,130 jobs. Together, the industry employment increases for *Job Printers, Desktop Publishers, Prepress Technicians*, and *Bindery Workers* accounted for only 12.7% of the gross increases in core printing occupations by industry.

Two occupations had the largest employment reductions by industry groups: *Bindery Workers* and *Prepress Technicians*. Job losses for these occupations totaled 53,260, and they were responsible for 55.8% of the gross reductions in core printing occupational employment by industry groups. Moreover, these two occupations had the smallest employment increases with a combined total of 1,360 jobs. This represents only 1.9% of the gross employment increases in all core printing occupations.

Employment Changes by Industry Groups

The substantial number of jobs that were added (reduced) by industry groups indicates that there were great differences between industry groups, both in the number of jobs created and in the number of jobs lost in core printing occupations. Figure 12 shows the gross employment increases in all core printing occupations by each of the major industry groups. The industries in the **Prof & Biz** group had the largest increases, adding 29,390 jobs and contributing 41.0% of the gross employment increases in core printing occupations by industry group. The **Prof & Biz** group created more than twice as many jobs (2.6:1) as the **PRINT** industry, which had the second largest increase. Combining the gross increases by the **PRINT** industry group with the industry groups that had the third and fourth largest increases among printing occupations with any employment gains, we find that 35.1% of all increases in employment by industry groups occurred in **PRINT**, **Publish**, and **W&R Trade**, with additions of 11,282 (15.8%), 6,968 (9.7%), and 6,850 (9.6%) respectively of the gross increases in employment by all industry groups. Hence, increases in printing occupational employment by the top four industry groups accounted for 76.1% of all such increases within industry groups.

Figure 12. Gross Employment Increases in All Core Occupations, by Industry Group, 2001–2005

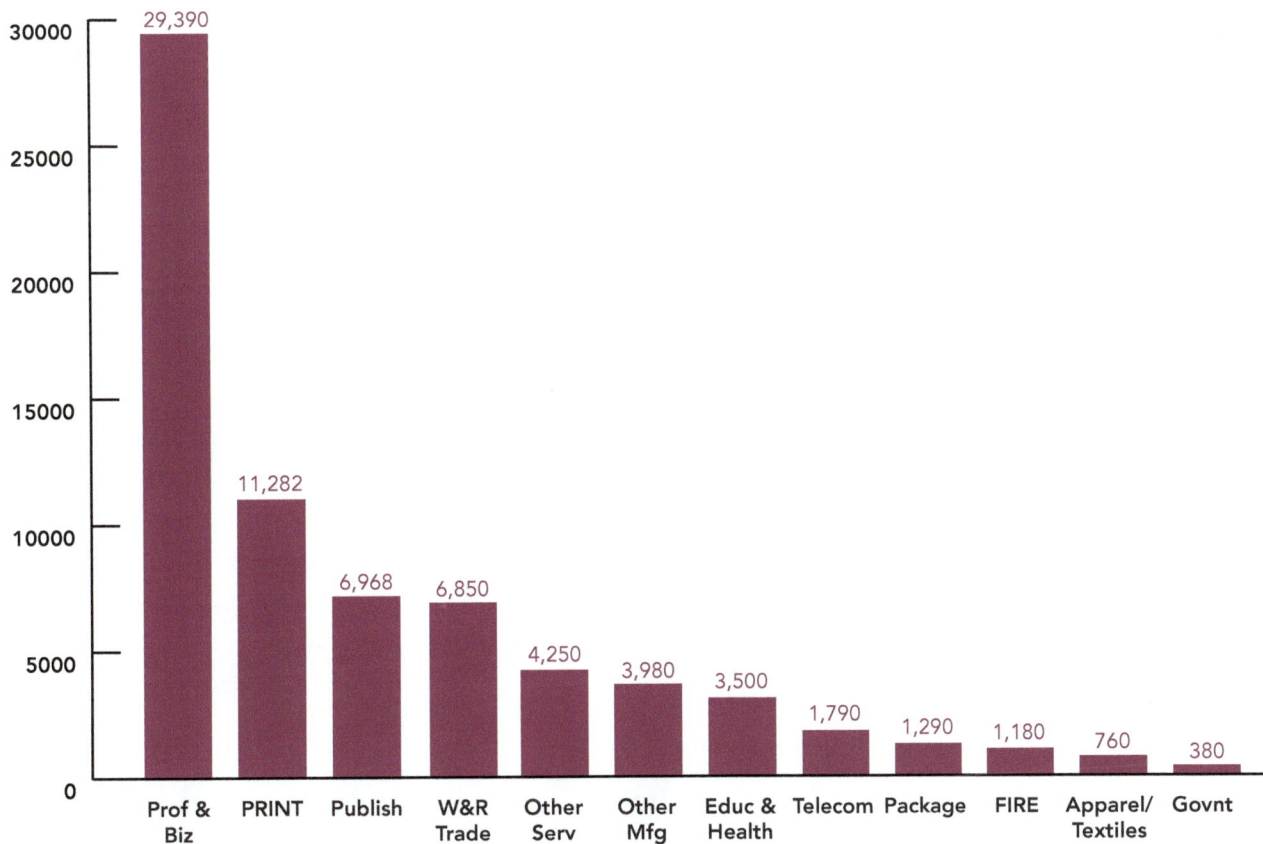

There were no increases in employment for any printing occupation by the construction and utilities industries (**NEC**), while two industry groups—**Apparel/Textiles** and **Govnt**—had fewer than 1,000 new jobs created in one or more printing occupations between 2001 and 2005.

Figure 13. Gross Job Losses for all Core Occupations by Industry Group, 2001-2005

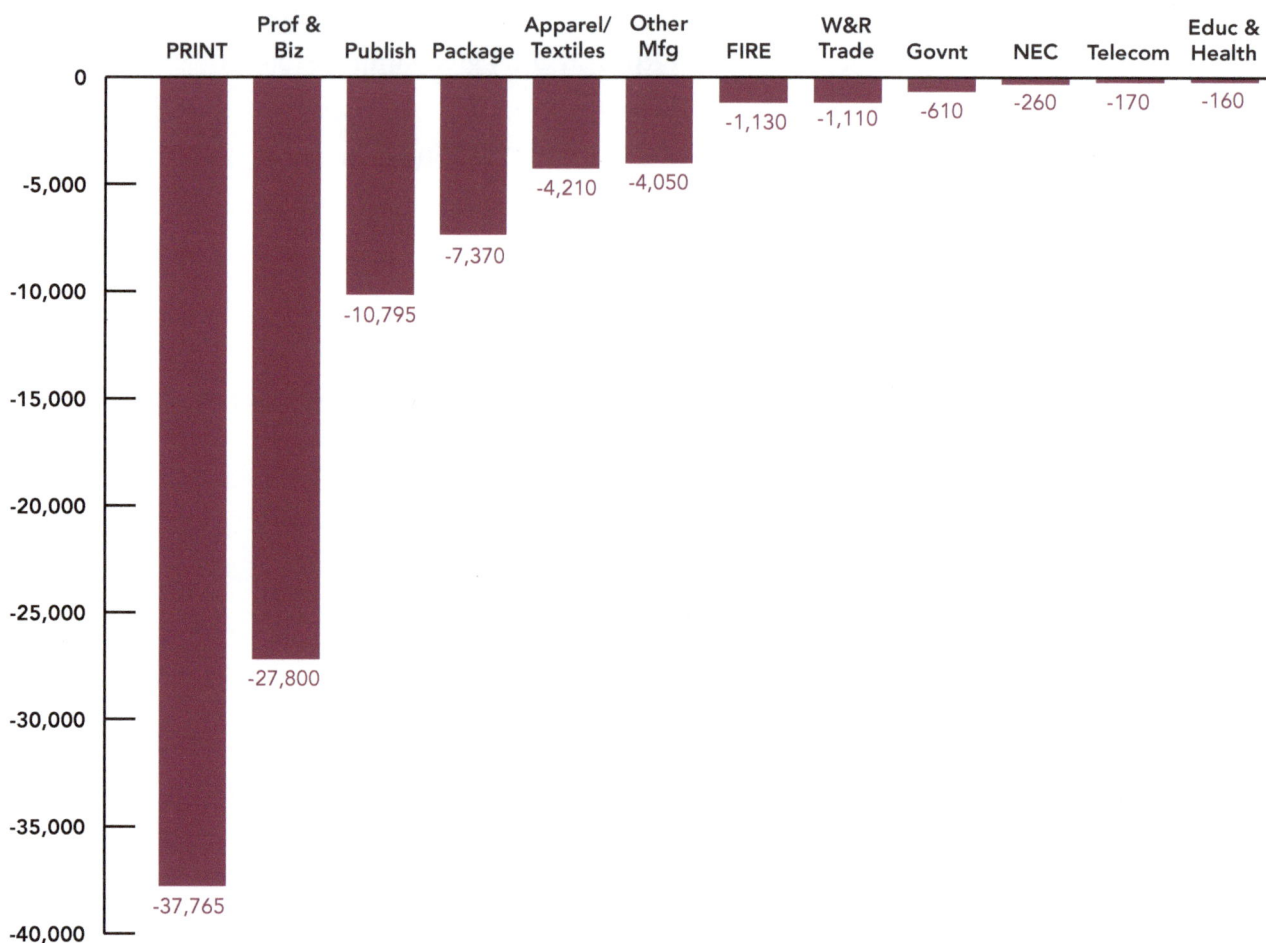

PRINT	-37,765
Prof & Biz	-27,800
Publish	-10,795
Package	-7,370
Apparel/Textiles	-4,210
Other Mfg	-4,050
FIRE	-1,130
W&R Trade	-1,110
Govnt	-610
NEC	-260
Telecom	-170
Educ & Health	-160

Just as the **Prof & Biz** group dominated industry groups' contributions to job creation, the **PRINT** industry dominated the job losses in printing occupations that occurred in all industry groups. With losses totaling 37,765, the **PRINT** industry was responsible for 39.6% of the gross reductions of employment in core printing occupations. **Prof & Biz** had the second largest reduction of 27,800 jobs for 29.1% of the total from all industry- and occupation-specific reductions. When compared to the **Publish** group, which had the third highest reductions of 10,795 jobs (11.3%), the reductions in the **PRINT** and **Prof & Biz** groups were much greater. For every job loss in **Publish**, there were 2.6 more in **Prof & Biz** and 3.5 more in the **PRINT** industry. Together, **PRINT** and the **Prof & Biz** group were responsible for 68.7% of all printing occupation-specific employment losses by industry groups. Missing from Figure 13 is the **Other Serv** group, which had no employment reductions in any core printing occupation between 2001 and 2005.

After adding increases (Figure 12) and decreases (Figure 13) for each industry group, the only industry groups with a net increase in total employment in all core printing occupations were **W&R Trade** (+5,740), **Other Serv** (+4,250), **Educ & Health** (+3,340), **Telecom** (+1,620), **Prof & Biz** (+1,590), and **FIRE** (+50). Within the **Prof & Biz** group[27], there were four subgroups that had net increases in employment (+29,066 jobs), and one

27 - The reason for the difference in **Prof & Biz** net increases (+1,590) as opposed to the subgroup net increases (a total of +1,320) is the issue of aggregation and disaggregation of the subgroups, as discussed on the next page.

subgroup with a substantial net loss of jobs (-27,476) in 2005. These subgroups are derived from disaggregating and re-combining the industries that comprise three clusters—**Adv & Design**, **Mgmt/Biz Support**, and **R&D/ Other Prof**— within the **Prof & Biz** group as described in Table 5. While the industries in the **Prof & Biz** group as a whole in 2001 are comparable to 2005, the individual SIC industry classifications used in 2001 do not permit the construction of the three clusters in their entirety. Thus, **Advertise** consists only of the advertising industry. However, there is no comparable industry for **Design** (NAICS 5414 Specialized Design Services) in SIC. Instead, the design industries are identified with more detailed classifications in certain business support services. [28] Thus, in combination with **Biz Support**, the subset **Biz Support & Design** includes a set of comparable industries for both periods.

In 2001, **Mgmt** refers solely to the SIC-based industries identified as specialties in managing other companies (holding companies and investment offices). In 2005, **Mgmt/HQ** (NAICS 5511 Management of Companies and Enterprises) includes these SIC classifications, a re-classification of a fraction of all other industries' employment in headquarter establishment, and *adds* an entire set of establishments that were previously excluded from all SIC industries.[29] As a result, employment increases in **Mgmt/HQ** reflect substantial additions of an entire category of establishments that was not previously counted as employment in any SIC classification. For these reasons, employment in **Mgmt/HQ** is identified as a separate sub-classification of the **Prof & Biz** group. Lastly, within the **R&D/Other Prof** cluster are industries that show substantially different patterns of employment growth for core printing occupations. To highlight these differences, the industries in this cluster are divided into two subgroups—**Computer Services** and **Other Prof**. The latter includes all other professional services in the **R&D/ Other Prof** cluster except computer services.

In the following sections on employment changes in specific occupations by industry group, the tables and ensuing discussion include a breakdown of the employment changes in the **Prof & Biz** group by these five sub-groups. Thus, in addition to **Telecom**, **W&R Trade**, and **Other Serv**, there are four groups of industries in **Prof & Biz**, with each one showing with a net increase in total employment in core printing occupations between 2001 and 2005. For **Advertise**, **Mgmt/HQ**, **Computer Services**, and **Other Prof**, the net increases were +13,350, +6,540, +4,840, and +4,336, respectively.

Design & Prepress Occupations

Overall, the national occupational employment data show a net increase in the number of workers in only one *Design & Prepress* occupation, the *Graphic Designer*. For the *Prepress Technician* and the *Desktop Publisher* occupations, there was an overall net reduction in employment between 2001 and 2005. Including the five comparable clusters in the **Prof & Biz** group, Table 14 shows the net employment changes from 2001 to 2005 in *Design*

28 - Design industries are included in SIC 733 (Mailing, Copying, & Reproduction services, Commercial Art & Photography, and Stenographic Services), and SIC 738, which includes all business services that do not have a separate 3-digit classification in SIC 73.

29 - An auxiliary refers to "Corporate, Subsidiary, & Regional Managing Offices". Employment in these establishments were not included in SIC industry employment totals. According to the report on the 1997 Economic Census, *Bridge Between NAICS and SIC*, 95% of the employment in NAICS 5511 (Management of Companies and Enterprises) is attributable to auxiliaries.

Table 14. Net Employment Changes in Design & Prepress Occupations by Industry Group, 2001-2005

Industry Group*	Net Change in Occupational Employment				Job Increases: % of Gross Total	Job Losses: % of Gross Total
	Graphic Designer	Desktop Publisher	Prepress Technician	All Design & Prepress		
Prof & Biz	12,850	1,720	-4,110	10,460	39.2%	26.3%
Advertise	5,810	1,100	-310	6,600	13.2%	0.8%
Computer Services	4,140	130	70	4,340	8.3%	--
Other Prof	4,230	20	-10	4,240	8.1%	0.03%
Mgmt/HQ	3,590	1,170	250	5,010	9.6%	--
Biz Support & Design	-4,920	-700	-4,110	-9,730	--	25.5%
W&R Trade	5,710	80	-580	5,210	11.0%	1.5%
Other Serv	2,680	790	130	3,600	6.9%	--
Other Mfg	3,220	200	-510	2,910	6.5%	1.3%
Educ & Health	2,800	200	-120	2,880	5.7%	0.3%
Telecom	1,760	-170	10	1,600	3.4%	0.4%
FIRE	790	260	10	1,060	2.0%	--
Apparel / Textiles	760	-50	-230	480	1.4%	0.7%
Govnt	210	100	-220	90	0.6%	0.6%
NEC	-170	--	--	-170	--	0.4%
Publish	6,428	-4,491	-2,365	-428	12.3%	18.0%
Package	1,220	-40	-1,660	-480	2.3%	4.5%
PRINT	4,602	-3,379	-14,145	-12,922	8.8%	45.9%
Column Totals	42,860	-4,780	-23,790	14,290	52,470†	-38,180†

*Industry groups are listed in rank order by the net increases (largest to smallest) in Design & Prepress occupational employment between 2001 and 2005.

† Gross totals of all job increases (or decreases) in selected occupations.

& Prepress occupations for seventeen industry groups. The groups are ordered (top to bottom) by the largest to the smallest increases in employment.

For *Graphic Designers*, employment increases occurred in fifteen of the seventeen groups, with reductions in two groups (**Biz Support & Design** and the **NEC** category). **Biz Support & Design** was responsible for 96.7% of all job losses by industry in the *Graphic Designer* occupation. Ten industry groups had net increases of employment in the *Desktop Publisher* occupation, while six reduced employment in this occupation. The job losses from industries with employment reductions exceeded the increases by other industries for a net reduction of 4,780 jobs in the *Desktop Publisher* occupation. The greatest job losses occurred in the **PRINT** and **Publish** industries, which accounted for 89.1% of all reductions in *Desktop Publishers*. While the reductions in **Package** (–40) and **Apparel/Textiles** (–50) were small, the result was the elimination of all jobs for the *Desktop Publisher* occupation in the two groups by 2005. Of the sixteen groups that employed *Prepress Technicians* in 2001, five had more workers in that occupation in 2005, adding a total of 470 new jobs. More than half (53.2%) of that increase occurred in **Mgmt/HQ**. The increase in *Prepress Technicians* by **Mgmt/HQ** was nearly twice that of the industry group with the second largest increase, **Other Serv**. In **Mgmt/HQ**, nearly all of the increases in employment between 2001 and 2005 reflect the change in definition of the industry. Thus, only 220 *new* jobs for *Prepress Technicians* were created by the growth of printing activity in **Other Serv, Computer Services, FIRE**, and **Telecom; Other Serv** and **Computer Services** contributed 90.9% of that growth. While there were small increases (10 new jobs) in **FIRE**[30] and **Telecom**, employment of *Prepress Technicians* in all other industries fell, resulting in 24,260 fewer jobs for the *Prepress Technician* occupation in these industries. By itself, the **PRINT** industry accounted for 58.3% of the gross job losses among *Prepress Technicians*.

For most industry groups, the number of new jobs for *Graphic Designers* was greater than the combined job losses in the *Desktop Publisher* and *Prepress Technician* occupations. Only five industry groups—**Biz Support & Design, PRINT, Package, Publish**, and **NEC**—show a net reduction of total employment in the *Design & Prepress* occupations. Within these five groups, there were 23,730 fewer workers employed in *Design & Prepress* occupations by these industries in 2005 than in 2001. The gross job losses by the five groups accounted for 94.3% of all industry-group reductions in *Design & Prepress* occupations.

PRINT contributed the greatest job loss (–12,922), with 54.5% of all net employment reductions by industry groups in *Design & Prepress* occupations. **PRINT** had the most losses in the *Prepress Technician* occupation, which accounted for 80.7% of **PRINT's** gross job losses and exceeded the reduction of *Desktop Publishers* in this industry group by 10,766 jobs. Following **PRINT, Biz Support & Design** contributed –9,730 reductions, accounting for 25.5% of all net employment reductions by industry groups in *Design & Prepress* occupations. However, in the **Biz Support & Design** industries, the greatest job loss occurred in the *Graphic Designer* occupation, which accounted for 50.6% of the gross losses in this industry group. The reduction of *Graphic Designers* exceeded the reduction of *Prepress Technicians* by 810 jobs.

While **Biz Support & Design** was the only group to have employment reductions in all three occupations,

---

30 - However, the increase in **FIRE**, although small, is significant because there were no *Prepress Technicians* employed in this industry group in 2001.

four industry groups had job *increases* in each **Design & Prepress** occupation. Job increases in **Mgmt/HQ, Computer Services, Other Serv**, and **FIRE** added 11,200 *Graphic Designers*, 2,350 *Desktop Publishers*, and 460 *Prepress Technicians*. In all, the thirteen industry groups with a net increase in employment of **Design & Prepress** occupations added 38,020 jobs. Excluding **Mgmt/HQ**, 33,010 jobs were created as a result of the expansion of *Design & Prepress* activity outside of the **PRINT** industry. Three industry groups—**Advertise, W&R Trade** and **Publish**—were responsible for 36.5% of the gross increases (+19,128 jobs). With respect to the net increase in jobs, five industry groups—**Advertise, W&R Trade, Computer Services, Other Prof**, and **Other Serv**—added 23,990 new jobs (72.7% of the total with the exception of **Mgmt/ HQ**).

Production Printers and Bindery Workers

National employment declined between 2001 and 2005 for both *Production Printers* (*Job Printers* and *Press Operators*) and *Bindery Workers*. Moreover, *Bindery Workers* had the greatest job loss/gross decreases by industry groups than any other core printing occupation (see Table 13), and there were only 890 new jobs created for *Bindery Workers* by industry groups (see Table 15). The occupation of *Job Printer* contributed 28.0% of job losses and 20.4% of gains in industry group employment of *Production Printers*. Overall, changes in the employment of *Job Printers* contributed 5.2% and 8.3%, respectively, of the gross increases and decreases by industry groups in all core printing occupations. By comparison, there were 3.9 jobs created for *Press Operators* as there were for each new *Job Printer* job. With respect to job losses among *Production Printers* as a whole, for every reduction in the *Job Printer* occupation, there were 2.6 fewer workers employed as *Press Operators* (a ratio of 1:2.6).

Table 15 shows the net changes in employment for each type of *Production Printer* and for *Bindery Workers*. For **Production Printers**, the table shows the industry group's share of both gross job increases and losses. For *Bindery Workers*, the table shows only the industry's share of job losses. From top to bottom, industry groups are arrayed by the largest net increase in employment to the largest net loss of jobs in the *Production Printer* occupations. With a net gain of 2,220 jobs, the **PRINT** industry had the largest increase in *Production Printers* among the twelve major industry groups. However, within **Prof & Biz**, there was a greater increase in the **Advertise** industry (+6,340). (This and the other job gains by **Computer Services, Other Prof**, and **Mgmt/HQ** were largely offset by the reductions of *Production Printers* by **Biz Support & Design** (–7,616).)

In all, the gross increase in employment of *Job Printers* by eight industry groups added 3,720 jobs. Three industries—**Advertise, Publish**, and **Other Mfg**—contributed 65.1% of that increase. For *Press Operators*, **PRINT** and **Advertise** had the largest increases in employment (6,680 and 5,020 jobs, respectively), followed by **W&R Trade** with 1,060 new jobs. Together, these three groups added 12,760 *Press Operators*, for 87.8% of all increases (+14,540 jobs). These gains were offset by the large job losses in both occupations in **Biz Support & Design, Package**, and **Apparel/Textiles**, with a net reduction of –17,216 *Production Printers*. Moreover, the employment gains for *Press Operators* in **PRINT, W&R Trade, Govnt**, and **FIRE** (+7,930 jobs) were accompanied by reductions in the employment of *Job Printers* (–6,020 jobs). Similarly, in **Publish** and **Other Mfg**, the increases in *Job Printers* (+1,100 jobs) were accompanied by employment losses for *Press Operators* (–4,920 jobs).

Six industry groups—**Advertise, Mgmt/HQ, Educ & Health, Other Serv, Computer Services**, and **Tele-**

Table 15. Net Employment Changes in Production Printers and Bindery Workers by Industry Group, 2001-2005

Industry Group*	Net Change in Occupational Employment				Percent of Gross Total		
	Press Operator	Job Printer	Bindery Worker	Production Printer**	Production Printer		Bindery Worker
					Increases	Losses	Losses
PRINT	6,680	-4,460	-15,781	2,220	36.6%	15.8%	54.4%
W&R Trade	1,060	-230	-300	830	5.8%	0.8%	1.0%
Prof & Biz	-150	710	-9,430	560	44.8%	27.01%	34.9%
Advertise	5,020	1,320	410	6,340	34.7%	--	--
Computer Services	130	210	160	340	1.9%	--	--
Other Prof	-4	60	40	56	0.3%	0.01%	--
Mgmt/HQ	910	530	90	1,440	7.9%	--	--
Biz Support & Design	-6,206	-1,410	-10,130	-7,616	--	27.0%	34.9%
Other Serv	330	200	120	530	2.9%	--	--
Educ & Health	200	300	-40	500	2.7%	--	0.1%
Telecom	20	--	--	20	0.1%	--	--
NEC	-90	--	--	-90	--	0.3%	--
Govnt	70	-220	-170	-150	0.4%	0.8%	0.6%
FIRE	120	-1,110	-20	-990	0.7%	3.9%	0.1%
Publish	-1,550	540	-2,389	-1,010	3.0%	5.5%	8.2%
Other Mfg	-3,370	560	-170	-2,810	3.1%	11.9%	0.6%
Apparel / Textiles	-3,530	-400	--	-3,930	--	13.9%	--
Package	-5,590	-80	70	-5,670	--	20.1%	--
Column Totals	-5,800	-4,190	-28,110	-9,990	18,260†	-28,250†	-29,000†

*Industry groups are listed in rank order by the net increase (largest to smallest) in Production Printers from 2001 to 2005.

**Production Printer represents the combination of Press Operators and Job Printers. Therefore, this column is the total of the increases (decreases) in occupational employment for the Press Operator and Job Printer columns.

† Gross total of all job increases (or decreases) in selected occupation(s).

com—had increases in the employment of *Production Printers* with no job losses. While the job gains were small in **Telecom** (+20), **Computer Services** (+340), **Educ & Health** (+500), and **Other Serv** (+530), **Advertise** and **Mgmt/HQ** were responsible for 42.6% of the gross increase in *Production Printers*, with the larger share of the increase occurring in the **Advertise** industry alone (+6,340 jobs).

Increases in an industry's employment of *Job Printers* that are accompanied by reductions in the number of *Press Operators* may reflect a shift in the responsibilities of workers who operate printing machines, as opposed to a loss of jobs. This is particularly true in small establishments where print operations are combined with short-runs and single copies. In such establishments, the printer has an expanded role in prepress and postpress tasks. Employment changes in two industry groups reflect such a shift in the role of printers. In **Publish**, the loss of 1,550 *Press Operators* and the increase of 540 *Job Printers* may indicate a shift in the types of printers (from *Press Operators* to *Job Printers*). Moreover, the net reduction in *Production Printers* by **Publish** may reflect downsizing of larger production printing operations that was accompanied by a relatively modest growth in printers' employment in small establishments. In 2001, there were no *Job Printers* reported to be employed in **Other Prof**, and the reduction of *Press Operators'* employment is quite small (–4 jobs). Hence, the increase in *Job Printers* is likely to reflect an increase in small-scale production operators in this group, rather than a shift in the in the skill requirements of *Production Printers* as appears to be the case in **Publish**. By contrast, the industry reductions in *Job Printers* in the **PRINT** industry may reflect greater job loss among small establishments. Considering the extent of industry reductions in *Prepress Technicians*, the employment losses in the *Job Printer* occupation may also reflect a net reduction in the demand for traditional skills in prepress work.

For *Bindery Workers*, modest increases in employment were confined to six industry groups—**Advertise**, **Computer Services**, **Other Serv**, **Mgmt/HQ**, **Package**, and **Other Prof**. In all, only 890 new jobs for *Bindery Workers* were created. The increase by the **Advertise** industry alone was responsible for 46.1% of these jobs. All other industry groups that employed *Bindery Workers* in 2001 reduced their workforces, with a gross loss of 29,000 jobs. The job losses in **PRINT** and **Biz Support & Design** were responsible for 89.3% of the gross reductions in *Bindery Workers*.

Expansion of Printing Activities in Other Industries

In the preceding section, the reductions in the employment of *Prepress Technicians* and *Bindery Workers* were attributed largely to the effects of technological changes on the tasks that workers perform in these occupations. The growth of digital printing and the expansion in the transmission of computerized print-ready layouts via the Internet have also affected the growth of employment in industries other than printing, particularly in the *Production Printer* occupations and the *Desktop Publisher* occupation. The gross changes in employment between 2001 and 2005 also provide an indication of the recency of each industry's involvement in printing activities.

We can examine the extent to which industries' design and prepress activities and print production in 2005 are largely the result of new hires by characterizing any employment increase in the relevant occupations by an industry group that occurred between 2001and 2005 as a "new hire." Since the employment increases in **Mgmt/HQ** reflect the creation of a new industry, derived in part from HQ employment in other industries and in auxiliary establishments that had not previously been included in industry employment statistics, the calculations of new hires exclude this industry. Thus, of the 580,620 workers employed in core printing occupations in all other industries, only 11.2% were new hires, reflecting the creation of 65,070 jobs by various industry groups. Figure 14 displays the percentage of 2005 employment identified as new hires for each industry group. Note that **Biz Support & Design** and **NEC** are not shown (in addition to **Mgmt/HQ**, as previously discussed), since there were no new hires in these groups for any core printing occupation.

Figure 14. Percentage of New Hires in All Core Occupations by Industry Group, 2005

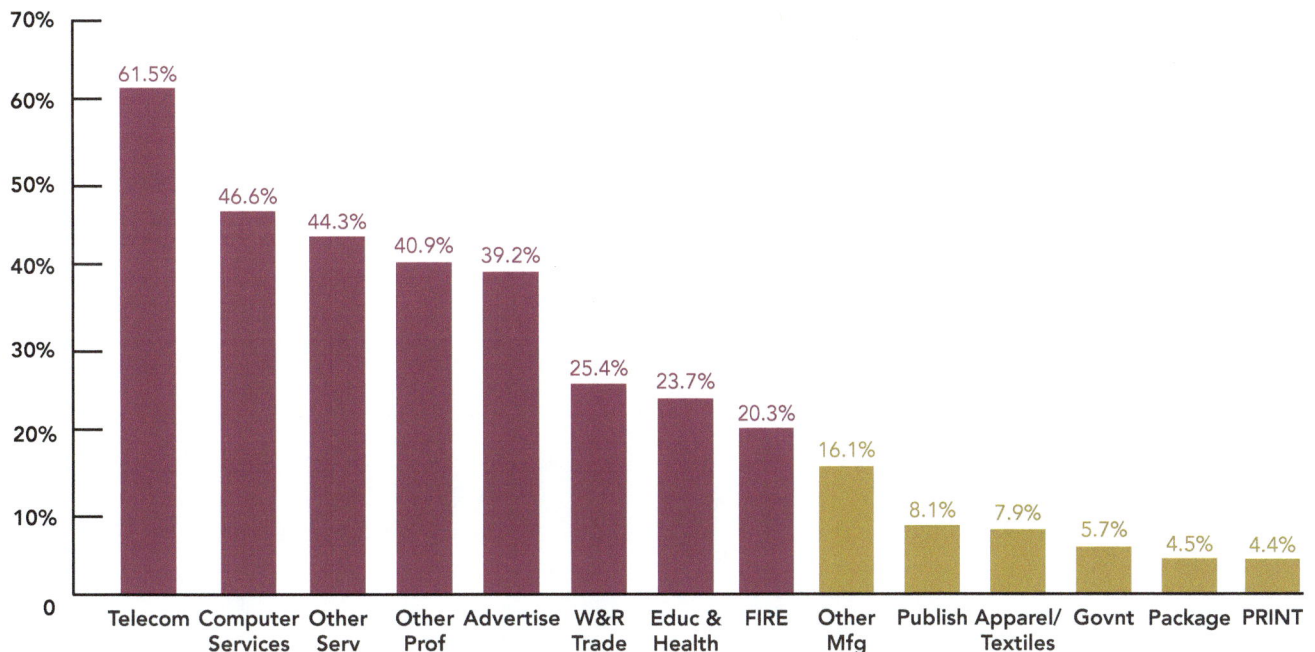

Industry groups that also had a net increase in employment are displayed as red columns; those in which job losses offset all increases, resulting in a net employment reduction, are shown as gold columns. Eight industry groups had a net increase in employment, and all eight had a higher percentage of new hires than the six industries with new hires that had an overall net reduction of employment in core printing occupations. Taken together, the high-growth industries (**Telecom, Computer Services, Other Serv, Other Prof, Advertise, W&R Trade, Educ & Health,** and **FIRE**) contributed 62.1% of all new hires by all industry groups. In 2001, these industry groups employed only 12.8% of workers in core printing occupations. With an overall employment growth rate of 51.6%, high-growth industry groups constituted 20.0% of 2005 employment in core printing occupations (115,926 jobs).[31] **Advertise** had the greatest increase (+13,660), contributing 33.8% of the gross increases in printing occupational employment by the eight industry groups, and 21.0% of the new jobs in all industry groups. **PRINT** added the second greatest number of new hires, with 11,278 jobs of the gross increases in employment. However, as a result of substantial job losses in certain occupations, **PRINT** had a net reduction of -9.4%.

31 - For consistency in making comparisons of industry shares, the 2001 count is computed without **Mgmt/HQ**. Only 270 workers were included in the industries identified as "managing other enterprises" in 2001. Employment in core printing occupations in all other industries totaled 610,950. In 2005, Mgmt/HQ employed 6,810 workers. Excluding these jobs, the 2005 employment in core printing occupations was 580,620.

Figure 15 shows the percentage of workers employed in *Design & Prepress* occupations in 2005 who were "new hires". As in Figure 14, **Mgmt/HQ** is excluded. Since there were no increases in any *Design & Prepress* occupations by **NEC** and **Biz Support & Design**, these industry groups are not shown. Industries with a net increase in *Design & Prepress* occupational employment, indicating an expansion of these activities, are shown in red. Note that only three industry groups—**PRINT**, **Publish**, and **Package**—had net reduction of employment in these occupations, and are therefore shown in gold. The industries with the highest rates of growth—**Telecom, Computer Services, Other Serv, Other Prof, Educ & Health,** and **W&R Trade**—were responsible for 47.9% of the gross increases in employment in *Design & Prepress* occupations, adding 22,750 new jobs. Still, this set of industries held only 24.5% of all employment in these occupations in 2005.

Figure 15. New Hires' Share of Industry Employment in Design & Prepress Occupations, 2005

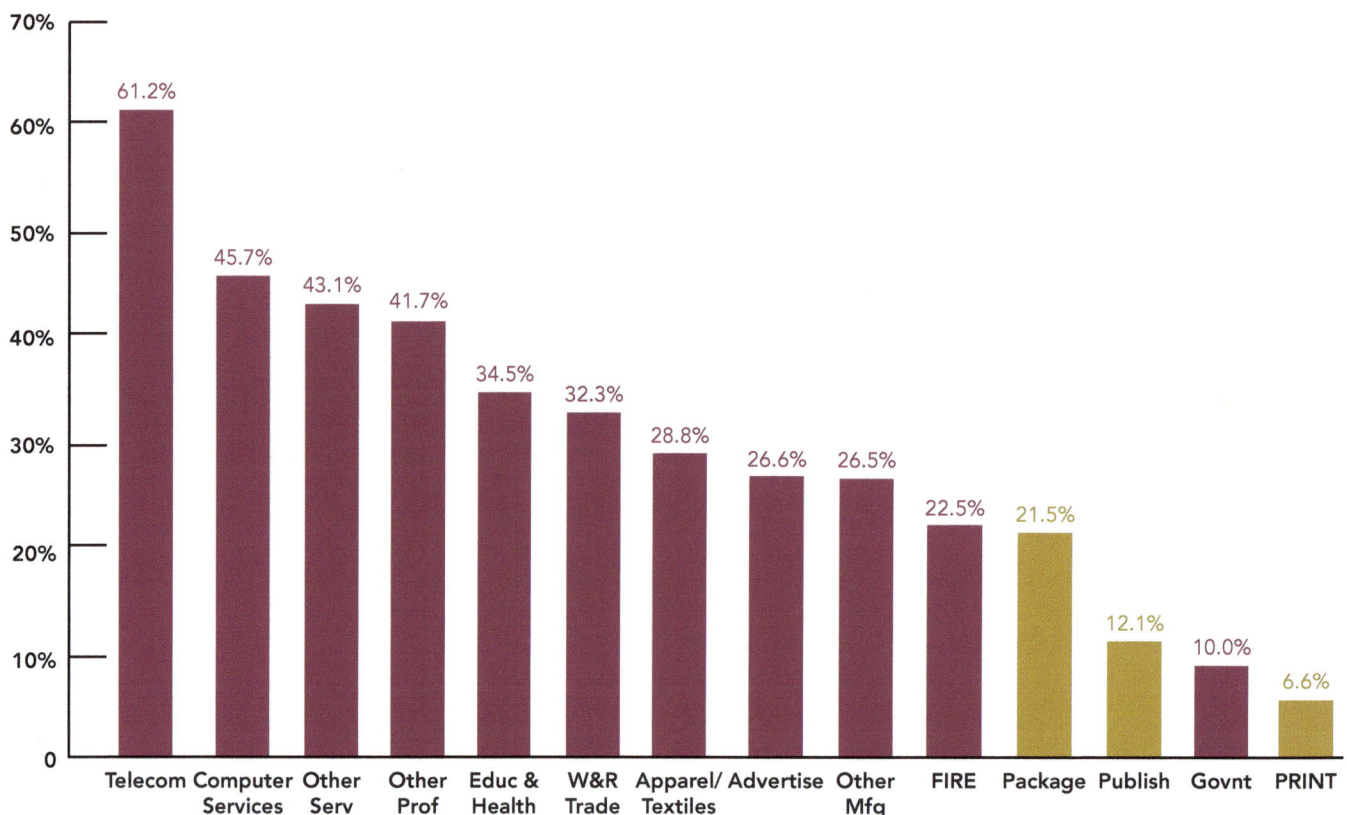

Of the total workforce employed in *Design & Prepress* occupations in 2005, 20.2% reflect new hires. In comparison to *Desktop Publishers* and *Prepress Technicians*, *Graphic Designers* had a much higher percentage of new hires, constituting 25.4% of the 2005 workforce in all industry groups (excluding **Mgmt/HQ**). Only 10.1% of *Desktop Publishers* and 0.3% of all *Prepress Technicians* employed by industry groups in 2005 can be attributed to industry-specific growth (new hires) in employment from 2001.

For the **PRINT** industry and other long-term producers of print materials, such as **Package**, **Apparel/Textiles**, and **Publish**, all of the increases in occupational employment related to the *Design & Prepress* stage were for *Graphic Designers*. All of the growth in employment of *Prepress Technicians* and *Desktop Publishers* occurred in other industries.

Employment growth for *Graphic Designers* constituted 93.5% of the gross increases in *Design & Prepress* occupations among the industries shown in Figure 15. The growth in employment of *Desktop Publishers* accounted for 6.1% of the increases, and *Prepress Technicians* made up the remainder (0.4%). For *Desktop Publishers*, **Advertise** alone was responsible for 38.2% of the increases, while the high-growth combination of **Other Serv**, **W&R Trade**, **Computer Services**, **Educ & Health**, and **Other Prof** contributed 42.4% of the new jobs. For the few new hires of *Prepress Technicians* (220), 90.9% of the growth occurred in **Computer Services** and **Other Serv**.

For the *Press Operator* and the *Job Printer*, new hires as a percentage of all industry-assigned jobs in 2005 were 7.1% and 6.4%, respectively.[32] However, new jobs for *Press Operators* constituted 81.0% of all new hires of *Production Printers*. Figure 16 shows all industry groups that had any employment increases in *Job Printers* or *Press Operators*. In addition to **Mgmt/HQ**, note that **Apparel/Textiles**, **Biz Support & Design**, and **Package** are excluded from the figure; the latter are industry groups with employment losses in both occupations. As in Figures 14 and 15, industry groups with a net loss of employment for *Production Printers* are shown in gold.

The high percentages of new hires by **Telecom**, **Advertise**, and **Computer Services** indicate the recent expansion of production activity by these industry groups. Taken together, these industry groups contributed 39.8% of all new jobs for *Production Printers*. However, the new hires in **Telecom** and **Computer Services** constitute only 2.1% of all new hires. As in the job growth for *Desktop Publishers*, **Advertise** contributed the most new jobs for *Production Printers* among high-growth industry groups with an increase of 6,340 jobs—79.2% of which occurred in the occupation of *Press Operator*. Among all industry groups with a net increase in *Production Printers*, the **PRINT** industry contributed the most new jobs (6,680).

While most of the *Production Printers* employed in **Other Serv**, **Other Prof**, **W&R Trade**, **Educ & Health**, and **Other Mfg** were not new hires, the 2,710 new jobs that were created indicate a further expansion of print production activity outside of the traditional print-producing industries. In all, 55.9% of the new hires for *Production Printers* reflects the expansion of print production in such industries. Including the growth in **PRINT**, there were 16,096 new jobs for *Production Printers* were created by industry groups that were expanding print production activities (shown in red in Figure 16).

32 - As in the previous discussion of new hires in *Design & Prepress* occupations, "all industry group" employment of *Production Printers* refers to total industry-group assigned employment minus **Mgmt/HQ**. For *Job Printers*, this total was 49,980 (50,510 less 530). For *Press Operators*, the total was 191,460 (192,410 less 950).

Figure 16. New Hires' Share of Industry Employment in Production Printer Occupations, 2005

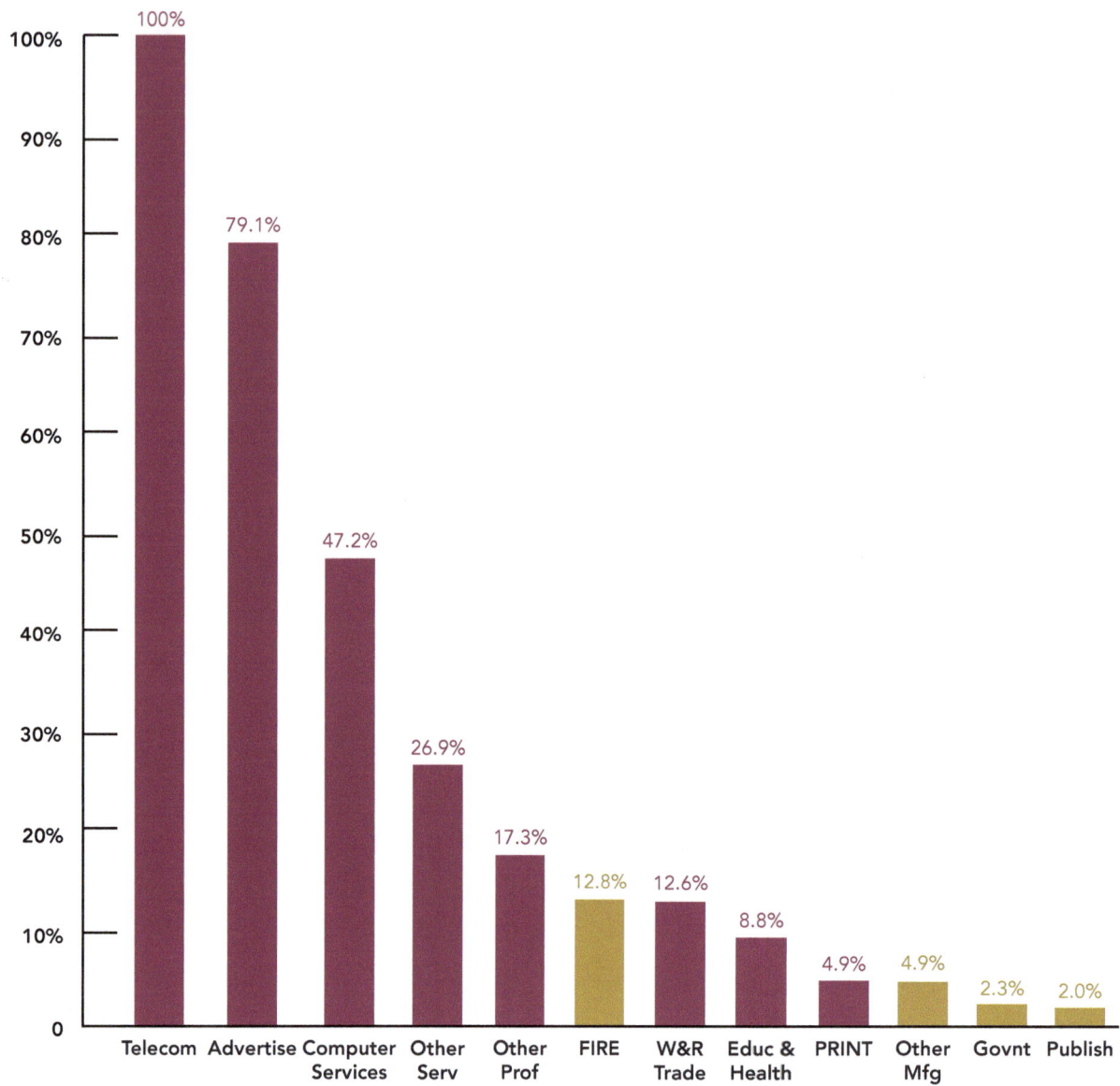

PRINTING OCCUPATIONAL EMPLOYMENT, HIGH-WAGE JOBS,
& INDUSTRY SOURCES OF GROWTH – 2001 TO 2005

Considering all the employment changes by industries, the overall pattern of decline in the employment of *Production Printers* that occurred in the U.S. economy as a whole is attributable largely to the reductions in employment that occurred in traditional print-producing industries, where there was a net loss of -10,610 jobs. In particular, the contraction of print production by **Publish**, **Package**, and **Apparel/Textiles** was responsible for 39.5% of the gross loss of jobs for *Production Printers* in all industry groups. Along with the job losses in the **Biz Support & Design** group, these four industry groups were responsible for 66.4% of the employment reductions of *Production Printers* by all industry groups (-18,766 of the gross total of -28,250). The analysis presented here suggests that expansion of print production was evident in eight other industry groups, and that much of that growth occurred within industries that did not have substantial production operations in 2001. Moreover, the industry pattern of employment changes in *Design & Prepress* occupational employment parallels that of production, with virtually the same set of industries responsible for most of the growth in employment between 2001 and 2005.

SECTION VI: FINAL OBSERVATIONS AND CONCLUSIONS

Shifts in Occupational Employment Related to Technological Change

Expanding Role of Graphic Designers

New printing technologies and the widespread use of sophisticated applications of graphic design for web-based displays and printing are having mixed effects on employment opportunities in the core printing occupations. In particular, much of the composition, layout, paste-up, and photography work performed by the traditional *Prepress Technician* can now be done with computer-based systems that involve the use of scanners, digital cameras, and software programs for formatting, illustrating and design, proofing, and color-separation. The two occupations most identified with the use of these technologies are the *Graphic Designer* and the *Desktop Publisher*. The *Graphic Designer* is responsible for planning and creating the design and layout of images and text of such printed documents as magazines and brochures, as well as printed material on packaging (paper, plastic, or metal), apparel and textiles, and cards. Both the *Graphic Designer* and the *Desktop Publisher* use computers in much of their work and must be familiar with as many as thirteen different software programs. Both are engaged in electronic composition and layout tasks using the same software programs, scanning machines, and digital cameras. Like the *Graphic Designer*, the *Desktop Publisher* creates graphics to accompany text, converts photographs and drawings into digital images, designs page layouts, and performs electronic typesetting and color separation. *Graphic Designers* have responsibilities that overlap with such desktop publishing occupations as 'electronic compositor or layout artist' and 'electronic image designer.'

Between 2001 and 2005, the overall demand for *Graphic Designers* from industry groups increased by 31.6%. While the demand for *Graphic Designers* was increasing in nearly all industries, there was a nearly universal reduction in employment in the traditional *Prepress Technician* occupation, with an overall decrease of 24.8%. During the same period, nine industry groups (including **Mgmt/HQ**) increased their employment of *Desktop Publishers*, adding 4,050 jobs. However, the employment reductions in six other industry groups were much greater, with a loss of 8,830 jobs. As a result, there were 13.8% fewer workers employed in desktop publishing jobs by industry groups in 2005 than in 2001. While 89.1% of the job loss in desktop publishing occurred in **PRINT** and **Publish**, two other traditional print-producing industry groups—**Apparel/Textiles** and **Package**—eliminated all desktop publishing jobs. The increases in the employment of *Graphic Designers* were substantially larger. For each eliminated job in the *Desktop Publisher* occupation, the number of new jobs created for *Graphic Designers* were 15 and 30 in **Apparel/Textiles** and **Package**, respectively.

Most of the increase in the employment of *Graphic Designers* occurred in industries other than the traditional print-producing industries. In all, **PRINT, Publish, Package**, and **Apparel/Textiles** contributed only 27.1% of that growth. Industries relatively new to printing with high percentages of 2005 employment in core printing occupations as the result of new hires include **Advertise, W&R Trade, Other Prof, Computer Services, Telecom, Educ & Health**, and **Other Serv**. Together, these industries were responsible for 56.6% of the growth in the employment of *Graphic Designers* between 2001 and 2005. Moreover, in both 2005 and 2001, *Graphic Designers* outnumbered *Desktop Publishers* and *Prepress Technicians* employed in each of these seven industries.

With respect to total employment in *Design & Prepress* occupations, *Graphic Designers* held 63.6% of these jobs in 2005 as compared to 50.9% of these jobs in 2001. The increasing importance of *Graphic Designers* suggests that much of the specialized electronic prepress work formerly performed by the *Desktop Publisher*, as well as some of the remaining tasks of the traditional *Prepress Technician* such as layout, composition, proofing, and photographic imaging, are being absorbed by the *Graphic Designer* occupation. Moreover, since the *Graphic Designer* creates web-site graphics, some of the increase surely reflects the increased business use of web-based advertising and on-line sales.

Industry Shifts in Occupational Employment of Production Printers

Between 2001 and 2005, the overall employment of *Press Operators* and *Job Printers* decreased by 3.1% and 8.4%, respectively. Three industry groups were responsible for 61.0% of the gross job loss in *Production Printer* occupations: **Package** (–20.4%), **Apparel/Textiles** (–13.9%), and **Biz Support & Design** (–27.0%). In all three industry groups, there were net reductions in both the number of *Press Operators* and the number of *Job Printers*. Together, these industries reduced employment of *Production Printers* by –17,216 jobs. However, the net reduction in *Production Printers'* employment by all industry groups totaled only –9,990 jobs.

While job losses of printers occurred in eleven industry groups, in seven industry groups job losses in one *Production Printer* occupation were accompanied by increases in the other.[33] Four industry groups (**Publish, FIRE, Govnt,** and **Other Mfg**) had a combined net job loss of –4,960 production printers. In **FIRE** and **Govnt,** employment losses in the *Job Printer* occupation (–1,330) were partly offset by increased employment for *Press Operators* (+190); whereas, in **Other Mfg** and **Publish**, the combined employment losses in the *Press Operator* occupation were –4,920, while there were only 1,100 new hires of *Job Printers*. Three other groups—**PRINT, W&R Trade** and **Other Prof**—had employment gains for one type of printer that were greater than the job losses in the other printer occupation, for a combined net gain of 3,106 *Production Printers*. In **PRINT** and **W&R Trade,** reductions for *Job Printers* totaled –4,460 and –230, respectively; whereas the employment gains for the *Press Operator* added 6,680 and 1,060 new jobs, respectively. In **Other Prof**, job losses for the *Press Operator* (–4) were accompanied by increases in employment for *Job Printers* (60).

With the expansion of new print production elsewhere and the net employment gains in **PRINT**, the loss of -10,280 *Production Printers* nationally can be largely explained by the contraction of print production activity in two of the traditional print-producing industries. With a combined loss of -9,600 *Production Printers*, **Apparel/ Textiles** and **Package** account for 96.1% of the net loss in *Production Printers'* employment that occurred between 2001 and 2005. While most of the job losses in **Apparel/Textiles** and **Package** may indicate a contraction of production, some of the losses reflect productivity improvements in print technology. The reductions in *Production Printers* within **Biz Support & Design** are more difficult to explain. These industries provide a wide variety of business services, including employment and payroll services, administrative services, and mailing, copying, and printing services. Thus, the reductions in *Production Printers* in these industries may reflect the unbundling of print production from these other services.

33 - In addition to the jobs losses for *Production Printers* in **Apparel/Textiles**, **Package**, and **Biz Support & Design**, the construction and utilities industries (**NEC**) eliminated all jobs for *Production Printers* (-90 *Press Operators*).

Industry-specific increases created 18,260 new jobs for *Production Printers*. Of that gross increase, 79.6% was attributable to the *Press Operator* occupation (14,540 new jobs). The **PRINT** and **Advertise** industries contributed the greatest number of new jobs for this occupation, adding 6,680 and 5,020 *Press Operators*, respectively. Moreover, **Advertise** also had the greatest share of new employment for *Job Printers*, accounting for 35.5% of the gross increase.

More often than not, the employment of *Job Printers* is associated with small-scale printing operations where the master printer is responsible for most (if not all) prepress, press operation, and postpress tasks. Five industry groups—**Computer Services, Other Prof, Educ & Health, Publish**, and **Other Mfg**—created more employment for the *Job Printer* than the *Press Operator* occupation. Taken together, new employment for *Job Printers* accounted for 83.7% of the gross increases in employment of *Production Printers* in these five groups. Hence, most of the growth in print production by these industry groups is likely to have occurred in small-scale print operations.

Outside the **PRINT** industry, the increases in *Production Printers'* employment signify the growth of new production activity by other industries. **Advertise**, which was responsible for 34.7% of the gross increases in *Production Printers'* employment, is providing printed advertising materials on a much greater scale in 2005 than in 2001, with new hires constituting 79.1% of 2005 employment.

The high rates of job growth for *Production Printer* occupations occurred in industries that also increased their *Design & Prepress* activity (particularly in the *Graphic Designer* occupation). However, among the industry groups with the highest overall rates of growth in core printing occupations—**Telecom** (61.5%), **Computer Services** (46.6%), **Other Serv** (44.3%), **Other Prof** (40.9%), and **Advertise** (39.2%)—there were substantially more jobs in *Design & Prepress* occupations than in printer occupations in 2005.[34] In 2005, the overall employment in core printing occupations in industries other than the traditional print-producing industries (i.e., **PRINT, Publish, Package**, and **Apparel/Textiles**) was still relatively small, accounting for 35.5% of the industry-assigned total (587,430). In particular, most *Production Printers* (78.4%) were employed in the above-mentioned traditional print-producing industries. Nevertheless, the net increases in employment of *Production Printers* in seven other industry groups suggest that print production activity is expanding outside the traditional print-producing industries.

In addition to software, changes in the hardware of printing machines have facilitated the growth of print production in industries other than the traditional print-producers. The growth in the use of "plateless" printing processes and computerization of machinery used in other printing processes make it possible (and economical) for businesses to operate in-house print production as well. "Plateless" or nonimpact printing processes, such as digital, electrostatic, and ink-jet printing, obviate the need for traditional plate-making tasks performed by *Prepress Technicians*, because these machines have the capability to "read" printable files which have been generated from the software that *Graphic Designers* and *Desktop Publishers* use. Depending on the scale of in-house print production where these machines are used, *Press Operators* will be employed to make adjustments related to the

34 - In 2005, employment in all *Design & Prepress* occupations ÷ employment of *Production Printers* was 3:1, 4:1, 13:1, 29:1, and 144:1 in **Advertise, Other Serv, Computer Services, Other Prof**, and **Telecom**, respectively. Among traditional print-producing industries, the highest ratio was in **Publish**, with 2 workers in *Design & Prepress* occupations for each *Production Printer* employed by the industry in 2005.

type of print medium, replace inks, install the paper or other printable materials that are required, monitor the machines and correct problems during a printing run. The increased use of computers, sophisticated sensors and instruments on printing machines used in the lithographic, flexographic and gravure printing processes allow for electronic (instead of manual) adjustments of press operations. As a result, many of the manual tasks that *Press Operators* used to perform have been "automated." As new generations of press technologies with such control system become widely used, operators will monitor press operations vis-à-vis a control panel and/or LCD displays and make adjustments electronically. With computerized systems, skills depend less on the "touch and feel" experience from handling the controls of a press, making a plate, and setting up a press. Instead, *Press Operators* must to be knowledgeable about computer systems, to have an understanding of the printing processes that are being monitored electronically, and to perform the programming necessary to control press operations.

Those business that have already begun to in-source marketing and design may find it advantageous to in-source print production as well. The amount of in-sourcing of print production will likely vary with an organization's size and printing needs. Thus far, such in-house print-production (as indicated by the employment of *Press Operators* and/or *Job Printers*) is relatively small in comparison to the extent of **Design & Prepress** activity in these industries. Far more difficult to predict is the extent to which the present business customers of the printing industry will increase their in-house capacity to print the materials that they are now purchasing from the printing industry.

Employment Growth in High-Wage Industries

In this study, high-wage employment is defined in relation to the wages of other workers in the same occupation. Hence, workers at or above the 75th percentile are paid wages that are higher than 75% of all workers employed in the same occupation. For each core occupation, a high-wage industry is one where the proportion of workers earning at or above the national 75th percentile wage is higher than the proportion with earnings below the national 25th percentile. Of the new hires in the *Graphic Designer* and *Desktop Publisher* occupations, 53% and 62%, respectively, occurred in high-wage industry groups. For the *Press Operator* and *Job Printer*, the shares of new hires that occurred in high-wage industries were 50% and 16%, respectively. Hence, for the occupations of *Desktop Publisher, Graphic Designer,* and *Press Operator*, at least half of all new hires occurred in industry groups with more high-wage than low-wage workers in these occupations. Only a small minority (16%) of new hires in the *Job Printer* occupation occurred in industry groups where there were relatively more high-wage than low-wage workers employed in that occupation in 2005.

In all industries, few new jobs were created for the occupations of *Bindery Worker* and *Prepress Technician*. Moreover, the vast majority of high-wage workers in these occupations were employed in industries with substantial job losses. The **PRINT** industry employed 86.3% of all high-wage workers in the *Bindery Worker* occupation (defined as 2005 wages greater than or equal to $32,000) and accounted for 54.4% of the job losses for that occupation. Similarly, the **PRINT** industry employed 62.8% of all high-wage jobs in the *Prepress Technician* occupation (2005 wages greater than or equal to $42,000), and contributed 58.3% of all job losses that occurred in that occupation between 2001 and 2005.

In 2005, there were nine industry groups in which the percentage of *Graphic Designers* with earnings at or above the 75th percentile (greater than or equal to $51,000) was greater than the percentage earning below the 25th percentile (less than $30,000). These high-wage industry groups—**Telecom**, **Advertise**, **Computer Services**, **Educ & Health**, **Other Prof**, **Other Serv**, **Package**, **FIRE**, and **Govnt**—contributed 23,640 new jobs for *Graphic Designers* between 2001 and 2005. (Of these, **Advertise, Other Prof**, and **Computer Services** were responsible for the majority of the new jobs (14,180) in high-wage industries.) Of the industry groups with relatively more high-wage than low-wage jobs in the *Desktop Publisher* occupation, four—**Computer Services, Other Prof, Other Mfg,** and **FIRE**—created a total of 610 new jobs between 2001 and 2005.

In 2005, the **PRINT** industry was the largest employer of both types of *Production Printers*, with 66.5% and 53.1% respectively of all *Job Printers* and *Press Operators*. Twenty-five percent of workers employed as *Production Printers* by the **PRINT** industry earned at or above the 75th percentile (greater than or equal to $40,000), while only 10% earned below the 25th percentile wage for the occupation. While **PRINT** did not have any new hires in the *Job Printer* occupation, the industry was responsible for the greatest number of new jobs in the *Press Operator* occupation. Of the 13,630 jobs identified as new hires of *Press Operators* since 2001, the **PRINT** industry alone was responsible for 49.0% of that growth.

Of the industry groups with more high-wage than low-wage employment in the *Job Printer* occupation, only two had any new hires. Together, **Other Serv** and **Educ & Health** had 500 new hires in the *Job Printer* occupation. In the industry with the greatest number of new hires of *Job Printers*, **Advertise**, 50% of those employed by the industry in 2005 were earning less than $25,000 (the 25th percentile low-wage threshold). One explanation for the preponderance of low-wage *Job Printers* in **Advertise** could reflect a concentration of small-scale printing operations in the industry.

Of the 65,070 new jobs in core printing occupations attributable to growth, high-wage employers contributed 31,250 new jobs in these occupations (48.4% of all new hires from 2001 to 2005). High-wage employment growth in the *Graphic Designer* occupation accounted for 75.0% of these jobs, a share that is greater than the overall importance of this occupation to employment increases in all core printing occupations by industry groups (66.9%). The *Press Operator* accounted for 20.3% of the gross increases in all core printing occupations and a comparable share of the new hires in high-wage industry groups (21.5%). The occupations with the fewest new hires—*Desktop Publisher* and *Job Printer*—had still smaller shares of the employment growth in high-wage industries, with 1.9% and 1.6%, respectively.

TECHNICAL APPENDIX—DATA AND METHODOLOGICAL ISSUES

TABLE OF CONTENTS

DATA SOURCES

The Occupational Employment Statistics Program (OES) provides annual estimates of employment in over 800 occupations for each MSA, each industry, and each state. These estimates are based on two sources of data: Surveys of establishments in all industries and an annual census of occupational employment in federal, state, and local government agencies. The OES does not collect occupational employment information from self-employed individuals.

The Standard Occupational Classification System

In 1999, the OES adopted a new occupational classification system. The Standard Occupational Classification (SOC) system has four levels of aggregation: Major and minor groups, and broad and detailed occupational categories. Each occupation in the SOC belongs to a single occupational group. In all, there are 23 major occupational groups. The major groups are divided further into 96 minor groups, 449 broad occupational categories, and more than 800 detailed occupations. Table A-1 displays a description and the SOC code for each major group.

Table A-1. Major Occupational Groups in the SOC

Group Code	Description
11-0000	Management Occupations
13-0000	Business and Financial Operations Occupations
15-0000	Computer and Mathematical Occupations
17-0000	Architecture and Engineering Occupations
19-0000	Life, Physical, and Social Science Occupations
21-0000	Community and Social Services Occupations
23-0000	Legal Occupations
25-0000	Education, Training, and Library Occupations
27-0000*	Arts, Design, Entertainment, Sports, and Media Occupations
29-0000	Healthcare Practitioners and Technical Occupations
31-0000	Healthcare Support Occupations
33-0000	Protective Service Occupations
35-0000	Food Preparation and Serving Related Occupations
37-0000	Building and Grounds Cleaning and Maintenance Occupations
39-0000	Personal Care and Service Occupations
41-0000	Sales and Related Occupations
43-0000*	Office and Administrative Support Occupations
45-0000	Farming, Fishing, and Forestry Occupations
47-0000	Construction and Extraction Occupations
49-0000	Installation, Maintenance, and Repair Occupations
51-0000*	Production Occupations
53-0000	Transportation and Material Moving Occupations
55-0000†	Military Specific Occupations

* These groups include at least one core printing occupation.
† No occupational estimates published for military occupations.

The SOC system consists of a six-digit classification. The first two digits identify major groups. Within each group, occupations may be differentiated by as many as four digits. Summary statistics on employment for each six-digit occupational classification in 22 of the 23 major occupational groups is available for each year. Approximately 50% of the pre-1999 detailed OES occupational classifications were carried forward into the SOC classifications. Unlike the U.S. Census, which has documented the connections between the SIC and NAICS industry classifications at a very detailed level in Report EC97X-CS3, *Bridge Between NAICS and SIC*, there is no comparable documentation for occupational data that shows how employment in the other 50% was divided among the new SOC categories.

As indicated in Table A-2, six occupations core to the printing process fall under three of the 22 groups for which published occupational employment data exist. New SOC occupational classifications (created in 1999) of importance to this study include *Graphic Designer* and *Prepress Technician*. In 1998 and earlier years, there were several classifications for specialized prepress occupations. The new *Prepress Technician* represents an aggregation of these specializations. However, the *Graphic Designer* occupation is a new six-digit classification that cannot be matched to specific classifications in the pre-1999 system. Hence, this analysis of printing occupations and changes in employment for each occupation was limited to the post-1998 period.

Table A-2. Core Printing Occupations in the Standard Occupational Classification System

SOC code	Occupational Title and Description	Illustrative Job Titles
27-1024	**Graphic Designers** Design or create graphics to meet specific commercial or promotional needs, such as packaging, displays, or logos. May use a variety of mediums to achieve artistic or decorative effects.	Catalogue Illustrator; Graphic Artist; Layout Artist
43-9031	**Desktop Publishers** Format typescript and graphic elements using computer software to produce publication-ready material.	Computer Compositor; Page Makeup System Operator
51-5011	**Bindery Workers** Set up or operate binding machines that produce books and other printed materials. Includes hand bindery workers. Excludes "Bookbinders" (51-5012).	Book Coverer; Stitching Machine Operator; Bookbinding Machine Operator
51-5021	**Job Printers** Set type according to copy; operate press to print job order; and read proof for errors and clarity of impression, and correct imperfections. Job printers are often found in small establishments where work combines several job skills.	Job Press Operator; Apprentice Job Printer
51-5022	**Prepress Technicians** Set up and prepare material for printing presses. Includes prepress functions, such as compositing, typesetting, layout, paste-up, camera operating, scanning, film stripping, and photoengraving.	Compositor; Lithographer; Photoengraving Etcher
51-5023	**Printing Machine Operators (Press Operator)** Set up or operate various types of printing machines, such as offset, letterset, intaglio, or gravure presses or screen printers to produce print on paper or other materials.	Bag Printer; Offset Press Operator; Lithoplate Maker

Annual Estimates of Occupational Employment by Industry

In order to provide *industry* estimates with a high degree of reliability, the OES has determined that a stratified random sample of 1.2 million establishments (by size categories, state, and industry) is optimal.[1] The universe of establishments (sampling frame) from which each sample is drawn are the list of all establishments that report to the State Employment Security Agencies for Unemployment Insurance (UI) purposes. Each quarter, the OES combines the data from all states into one file. A permanent random number (PRN) is assigned to every establishment in the file that is maintained by the OES. Hence, only "new" establishments (those that have been established since the last quarter) are assigned a new PRN. The file maintained by OES is referred to as the Longitudinal Data Base (LDB). Since nearly all businesses are required to file these reports in the state where they are located (exceptions are railroads and state, local, and federal government agencies), the LDB constitutes the universe of business (and not-for-profit) establishments in the U.S. In 2003, there were approximately 6,500,000 establishments identified in the LDB.

Over a three-year cycle, 1.2 million establishments are surveyed. For establishments with fewer than 250 employees, probability sampling is the basis for selection within a size category. Establishments with 250 or more employees are "certainty" units and **all** such establishments are surveyed once during each three-year cycle. Using the PRN assigned to each establishment, the OES ensures that those with fewer employees will be surveyed more than once during each three year cycle.

Since November of 2002, the OES surveys one-third of these establishments in two biannual surveys of 200,000 establishments, which are conducted in May and November. Prior to 2002, one annual survey of 400,000 establishments was conducted each year. Since 2002, the OES produces estimates for 350 four- to five-digit industries, each Metropolitan Statistical Area (a total of 334 MSAs), by size of establishment. Each sample is stratified by MSA (334), industry (350), and employment size of the establishment (seven size categories: 1-4, 5-9, 10-19, 20-49, 50-99, 100-249, and 250 + employees).

For each reporting period, the OES provides a list of establishments to be surveyed, survey forms, and procedural guidelines to each state's employment security agency. Each agency is responsible for mailing the survey to all establishments in the state's sample, conducting follow-up mailings and telephone calls to non-respondents, and compiling the data that are subsequently submitted to the OES for analysis.

Table A-3 shows the sample sizes for each year that were used to construct occupational employment estimates for 2000, 2001, and 2005. The samples for 2000 and 2001 are not independent. Two-thirds of the sample establishments used to estimate occupational employment in 2001 constituted 100% of the 2000 sample. With the exception of certainty units (establishments with more than 250 employees), the probability sample in 2005 is independent of the samples used in 2000 and 2001.

---

1 - This discussion of sample size and survey methods is based on the following documents: "Appendix B: Survey Methods and Reliability of the 2000 Occupational Employment Statistics Estimates," *Occupational Employment and Wages, 2000, Bulletin 2549*, U.S. Department of Labor, April 2002; "Technical Notes for OES Estimates," www.bls.gov/oes/2002/oes_tech. htm; and "Technical Notes for November 2004 OES Estimates," www.bls.gov/oes/current/oes_tech.htm.

Table A-3. Source Samples of Occupational Employment Estimates for 2000, 2001, and 2005

Survey period	Approximate sample size each period	2000		2001		2005	
		Total Sample	Cumulative Percent	Total Sample	Cumulative Percent	Total Sample	Cumulative Percent
1999	400,000	400,000	50.0%	400,000	33.3%		
2000	400,000	400,000	**100.0%**	400,000	66.7%		
2001	400,000			400,000	**100.0%**		
Nov-02	200,000					200,000	16.6%
May-03	200,000					200,000	33.3%
Nov-03	200,000					200,000	50.0%
May-04	200,000					200,000	66.7%
Nov-04	200,000					200,000	83.3%
May-05	200,000					200,000	**100.0%**
Total sample size		**800,000**		**1,200,000**		**1,200,000**	

Assessment of Missing Industry Detail in 2000 and 2001

All industries with any employment in a particular occupation are identified in the OES data. If an industry count has been suppressed, the symbol '**' will be reported. When an industry has no employment in a particular occupation, there will be no record of that occupation in the industry. Thus, the list of industries with a record for each core occupation is complete.

Like the occupational classification system, industry classifications are hierarchical. Thus, in the SIC system that was in use by the OES prior to 2002, major industry classifications are defined at the two-digit level. Within each two-digit industry group, are found more detailed classifications. While detailed industry classifications may have as many as eight digits, occupational employment estimates were only available for the two- and three-digit classifications in 2001. The sample sizes for 2000 and 2001 are both sufficiently large enough to be considered as a potential base year for comparisons to 2005 industry employment for the selected core occupations. Several issues were of importance in choosing 2001 as the base year. Those concerning the business cycle are discussed at length in Section V of the report. Here, we focus on the problem of missing data on industry estimates of occupational employment. As indicated in Table A-4, in both 2000 and 2001, the industry-specific counts were less than the national occupational employment for each occupation of interest. In each year, more than 21,000 jobs were not assigned to a specific three-digit SIC industry. The problem of missing industry assignment was greatest for the occupations of *Desktop Publisher, Job Printer,* and *Press Operator.*

Table A-4. Occupational Employment with No Industry Assignment in 2000 and 2001

Occupation	Jobs Not Assigned to any Industry Group*			
	2000	% Of All Jobs	2001	% Of All Jobs
Graphic Designer	2,820	2.1%	2,900	2.1%
Remaining - no industry†			840	0.6%
Desktop Publisher	1,620	4.6%	1,690	4.8%
Remaining - no industry†			290	0.8%
Prepress Technician	1,450	1.4%	3,680	3.8%
Remaining - no industry†			840	0.9%
Press Operator	9,830	4.6%	6,730	3.4%
Remaining - no industry†			500	0.3%
Job Printer	2,760	5.5%	4,770	8.6%
Remaining - no industry†			510	0.9%
Bindery Worker	2,930	2.9%	1,940	2.1%
Remaining - no industry†			850	0.9%
All Core Occupations	21,410	3.3%	21,710	3.5%
Remaining - no industry†			3,830	0.6%
Total Employment, All Core Occupations	640,980		615,070	

*For each occupation, jobs not assigned to any industry = National occupational employment − ∑industry-assigned jobs, for all 3-digit SIC industry classifications.

†Jobs that could not be classified as belonging to a particular industry group, by comparing 2-digit SIC totals with counts of all jobs in 3-digit SIC classifications. Employment data by 2-digit SIC were available for 2001 only.

For 2000, no additional information on industry employment in these occupations was available; whereas, in 2001, occupational employment was also reported for the two-digit industry classifications. As a result, it was possible to make adjustments to "industry-group" counts for 2001. Many industry groups include all of the industries in a two-digit classification. In such cases, the two-digit SIC occupational employment total was assigned to the industry group. Industry groups in this category include **Apparel/Textiles**, **Educ & Health**, **Govnt**, **W&R Trade**, **FIRE**, **Other Mfg**, **Other Serv**, and **NEC**. Because some two-digit totals were suppressed, it was not always possible to construct a complete total. Thus, for example, in SIC 48 (Communications), there were few *Prepress Technicians* and the overall count was suppressed. Since there were also no counts reported at the three-digit level, no employment of *Prepress Technicians* was estimated for the **Telecom** group. However, for the *Desktop Publisher*, there was some employment reported in SIC 792 (Theatrical Producers, except Motion Picture), while the count was suppressed at the two-digit level (SIC 79, Amusement and Recreation Services). Since there were employment counts in other two-digit industries, it was possible to compute an overall estimate for the **Other Serv** group. When the two-digit count was greater than the sum of all three-digit industries in the same two-digit classification, the two-digit count was substituted and the three-digit industry counts were adjusted for those three-digit industries assigned to different industry groups. By using such procedures, it was possible to reduce the missing industry counts for core printing occupations in 2001 by 82%. However, it was not possible to achieve an exact match between the national occupational employment total with the total from all industry groups. This was due to some missing industry counts at the two-digit level in several industries, as well as to rounding errors.

Missing Industry Counts in 2005

Beginning in 2002, the OES published occupational employment data by industry using the NAICS system. Therefore, for 2002 and later years, the OES published occupational employment for each four-digit industry in the NAICS. In 2005, the OES provided job counts at two higher levels of aggregation (three-digit and two-digit NAICS codes). As a result, it was possible to reduce the impact of missing industry assignments on the 2005 estimates of occupational employment by industry group as well. Table A-5 shows the national employment, the total employment reported at the four-digit level of the NAICS, and the final counts for all industry groups for each core printing occupation. For the latter two estimates of occupational employment, the table shows the number of jobs that were not assigned to an industry or industry group.

Table A-5. Occupational Employment Estimates for 2005 from Industries (4-digit) and Industry Groups with Missing Industry Counts

Occupation	National Total	Industries' Count	% Of National	Industry Groups	% Of National
Graphic Designer	178,530	176,000		178,490	
Missing Industry†		2,530	1.4%	40	0.02%
Desktop Publisher	29,910	27,390		29,790	
Missing Industry†		2,520	8.4%	120	0.4%
Prepress Technician	72,050	70,400		71,950	
Missing Industry†		1,650	2.3%	100	0.14%
Press Operator	192,520	186,270		192,410	
Missing Industry†		6,250	3.2%	110	0.06%
Job Printer	50,580	48,130		50,510	
Missing Industry†		2,450	4.8%	70	0.14%
Bindery Worker	64,330	61,760		64,280	
Missing Industry†		2,570	4.0%	50	0.08%
All Core Occupations	587,920	569,950		587,430	
Missing Industry†		17,970	3.1%	490	0.08%

† For each occupation, the calculation of missing industry counts for "Industries' Count" is as follows: Total jobs missing industry assignment = National occupational employment − ∑Industry-assigned jobs, for all 4-digit NAICS industry classifications. The total number of jobs missing an industry group assignment ("Industry Groups") = National occupational employment − ∑industry group employment with adjustments based on 3-digit and 2-digit NAICS industry counts.

In 2005, the percentage of national employment in core printing occupations that was not assigned to a specific four-digit NAICS classification was 3.1%. In both 2000 and 2001, the percentages were higher, and there were 3,740 fewer jobs that lacked an industry assignment in 2005 than in 2001. After adjusting industry group counts with data available from NAICS three- and two-digit totals, there were only 490 jobs lacking an industry group assignment in 2005, compared to 3,830 in 2001.

In 2001 and 2005, the two-digit level of industry classification was the most aggregated level for industry employment by occupation. In 2005, the greater reduction in missing industry counts was achieved because only two of the two-digit NAICS classifications suppressed employment in any core printing occupation. Moreover, only four of the six core printing occupations had a suppressed industry count at this level. There were no suppressed counts for the occupations of *Graphic Designer* and *Bindery Worker* at the two-digit level. Of the four occupations with suppressed industry counts in 2005, three (*Prepress Technician, Press Operator,* and *Job Printer*) had suppressed employment in the same two-digit industry, while another industry had suppressed the count employment for the *Desktop Publisher* occupation.

By contrast, in 2001, there was at least one two-digit SIC classification with suppressed job counts for each of the six core occupations. While the *Bindery Worker* and *Prepress Technician* occupations each had one suppressed (two-digit) industry count, the other core printing occupations had suppressed counts in two or more industries. Two suppressed industry counts were identified for the *Graphic Designer* and *Desktop Publisher* at the two-digit level. For the *Job Printer* and *Press Operator,* the number of two-digit industries with suppressed counts were three and five, respectively. In all, there were 13 two-digit SIC classifications with suppressed counts for one or more core printing occupations.

INDUSTRY GROUPS FOR 2001 AND 2005

Industry Groups Composed of Related Industries

Ten industry groups—**PRINT**, **Package**, **Apparel/Textiles**, **Publish**, **Prof & Biz**, **Educ & Health**, **W&R Trade**, **FIRE**, **Telecom**, and **Govnt**—are composed of industries that are related to one another either by type of product (or service) or by similarities in the use of printing in their production processes. Three categories—**Other Mfg**, **Other Serv**, and **NEC**—are combinations of industries in which no subgroup was a particularly important employer. **Other Mfg** and **Other Serv** refer to all the remaining industries in the manufacturing and service sectors, respectively. **NEC** is a residual category for all other industry sectors, such as construction, mining, agriculture, and utilities. In describing the differences (and similarities) between SIC- and NAICS-defined industry groups, only those groups composed of closely-related industries are discussed in detail.

Differences in Industry Classification Schemes

In 1997, the U.S. replaced the Standard Industry Classification (SIC) system with the North American Industry Classification System (NAICS). Although some classifications remained the same, the NAICS also created 358 new industry classifications and eight new sectors. Entire industry groups that were previously classified in manufacturing were moved to new non-manufacturing sectors. Moreover, at the detailed level, some NAICS manufacturing classifications now combine activities that had been previously assigned to separate SIC classifications. In some instances, these changes represent a reshuffling of activities among related industries. In others, the new NAICS classifications are not so easily decomposed, since they reflect a combination of activities that were previously treated as unrelated and were assigned to different industry groups within the SIC system.

The NAICS includes new industries and sectors that combine SIC classifications which do not belong to the same two-digit industry. There are a number of new NAICS classifications at the four-digit level for which there are no comparable SIC classifications, even at a very detailed level. For example, "Specialized Design Services" (NAICS 5414) includes some of the establishments in SIC 738 (Miscellaneous Business Services) that specialize in "Interior & Industrial Design, and Other Design Services" and, at the four-digit level, all of SIC 7336, "Graphic Design & Commercial Art."

The Economic Census of 1997 reports employment by both the NAICS and the SIC and provides tables that show the contribution to each NAICS classification from each source SIC. The SIC-bridge tables show the total employment for each three-digit SIC and provides a detailed breakdown (by four- and five-digit SIC) of the distribution of the total among the NAICS industry classifications. Excluded from the Census are those education industries which are dominated by public institutions. For all other industries, it is possible to identify the major contributing SICs for each NAICS classification, as well as how much employment from each three-digit SIC was assigned to a particular NAICS classification.

Sources of Information on Industry Composition

In 2001, all industry groups of related industries include multiple three-digit SICs. Moreover, with the exception of the printing industry (NAICS 3231), all other NAICS-defined industry groups include multiple four-digit

NAICS classifications in 2005. For 2001, the most detailed industry classification consists of three-digit SICs. In 2005, the four-digit NAICS industry serves as the building block for each industry group. Thus, the definition of an industry group was expanded (or contracted) to achieve the closest possible fit in terms of industry composition and employment. Some industry groups are composed of identical SIC and NAICS industries. While the code and the number of digits may not be the same, it was possible to identify a unique combination of SIC-defined classifications that were equivalent to the industry composition of the NAICS-defined group. However, an exact match was not possible for most industry groups.

Since the industry detail was so limited in 2001, the best fit constructed from the SIC data was rarely an exact match to the NAICS-defined group. The construction of comparable industry groups was made with the aid of a government report (EC97X-CS3) entitled *Bridge between NAICS and SIC*. The report provides employment counts for each SIC included in an NAICS classification at a very detailed level. Data from the 1997 and 2002 Economic Census was also used to construct comparable industry employment estimates for certain SIC-defined industry groups when the three-digit detail was insufficient. Since the BLS industry employment data is the one source with employment for the major educational industry categories (universities and colleges, primary and secondary schools), the author relied on the 2001 BLS industry employment data to assess the relative importance of those education industries which were included in the Economic Census.

The following sections provide a detailed description of the SIC- and NAICS-defined industry groups, identify the degree to which a NAICS industry group is inclusive of the SIC-defined group, and discuss major discrepancies between the two. For certain industry groups, only the aggregate employment is equivalent. In other industry groups, there are some "clusters" of industries that are equivalent, while total employment in the SIC-defined group composed of three-digit SIC classifications is not an exact match to the total employment identified with the NAICS group constructed from four-digit NAICS industries.

Industry Groups with Equivalent Industry Composition

There are several industry groups that have the same industry classifications and nearly equivalent employment in both the SIC and NAICS systems. Since the BLS defines government administration at the federal, state, and local levels as a separate category, no changes were made in the definitions of **Govnt**. **W&R Trade** remains largely intact in the SIC and NAICS systems. In both the SIC and NAICS definitions, **Package** is constructed from the same combination of industries that are inclusive of packaging: bags, boxes, bottles, and wrappings made of paper, plastic, and glass. The **Apparel/Textiles** group is inclusive of all industries in apparel, textiles, and leather goods manufacturing. While there were some re-classifications of employment in SIC classifications within apparel manufacturing, all but a tiny fraction of textiles, shoes, and other leather goods are inclusive of the same set of industries in both SIC and NAICS. Although there is no one-to-one correspondence of the SIC and NAICS classifications in **Telecom**, the combination of SIC classifications account for 100% of the NAICS-defined group.

Telecom

The composition of the SIC-defined **Telecom** is equivalent to its NAICS counterpart. Table A-6 shows that all of the source SICs and all of the employment in the NAICS-defined group are included in the SIC-definition of **Telecom**. The 2005 occupational employment data for **Telecom** are identified with two 3-digit classifications: NAICS 515 and 517. These classifications were first created in the Economic Census of 2002. In order to create a comparable group from the SIC classifications identified in the 1997 Bridge table, it was necessary to convert the classifications in NAICS 515 and 517 back to the sources in NAICS 513. Table A-6 shows the NAICS 515-517 industry distribution of 1997 employment based on 2002 shares of employment that were used to create these industries from the "old" NAICS 513. All employment in NAICS 515 and 517 can be traced to the source SICs identified in the table. While the overall group is equivalent, it is not possible to compare the subgroups of broadcasting and telecommunications directly.

Table A-6. NAICS and SIC Industries in Broadcasting and Telecommunications (Telecom)

% NAICS Group	NAICS Group Employment	Industry Description	NAICS	SIC Group % of Total	% SIC Group	SIC	SIC Group Employment	Industry Description	% in NAICS Group	5151	5152	5171	5172	5173	5174	5175	5179
	1,434,455			100%			1,450,043		99%	8.7%	10.3%	56.2%	10.1%	2.1%	0.8%	10.2%	0.5%
19.3%	276,203	Broadcasting (except Internet)			29.2%		424,066	Radio and television broadcasting	100%								
		Industry Description	NAICS			SIC		Industry Description									
		Radio Broadcasting	5151			483		Radio and television broadcasting		50.7%	49.3%						
		Television Broadcasting	5152			484		Cable and other pay television broadcasting	100%	15.2%						84.8%	
80.7%	1,158,252	Telecommunications		100%	70.8%		1,025,977	Telecommunications	98.5%								
		Industry Description	NAICS			SIC		Industry Description									
		Wired telecommunications carriers	5171			481		Telephone	98.8%			81.4%	14.4%	3.0%			
		Pagers, cellular phones & other wireless communications	5172			482		Telegraph communications	100%			100%					
		Telecommunications resellers	5173			489		Communication services, n.e.c.	85.6%				9.6%		48.6%		27.3%
		Satellite telecommunications	5174														
		Cable & other program distribution	5175														
		Other telecommunications	5179														

% of Total in NAICS Classification

Wholesale and Retail Trade

In the SIC system, the wholesale and retail trade industries are identified at the two-digit level. Wholesale durable and non-durable goods are classified in SIC 50 and 51, respectively. Retail trade industries are inclusive of SIC 52-9. The overall set of industries identified in Table A-7 is comparable in terms of overall employment (with less than 1% difference), as are many of the detailed industry classifications. Only a small percentage of industry employment in SIC 51, 54, 56, 57 and 59 was re-classified, and this was largely to manufacturing industries.

In the NAICS, 12.9% of the SIC-defined wholesale trade-durable goods (SIC 50) was re-classified as retail trade, and 7.0% of non-durable wholesale trade employment (SIC 51) was defined as retail trade. Moreover, all of SIC 58, "Eating and Drinking Places", is excluded from the NAICS definition of retail trade industries and assigned to a new industry, "Food Services and Drinking Places" (NAICS 722). Including NAICS 722 in the definition of **W&R Trade** results in a set of NAICS classifications that are comparable to the SIC definition.

Table A-7. NAICS and SIC Industries in Wholesale and Retail Trade (W&R Trade)

NAICS

NAICS	NAICS Group Employment / Industry Description	SIC Group % of Total	SIC Group Industries % of Total 50-51	SIC Group Industries % of Total 52-57, 59
	27,542,227	99.9%		
% NAICS Group 21.0%	Wholesale Trade			
	5,796,557	99.8%		
	Industry Description			
4211-4219	Wholesale durable goods	99.7%		
4221-4229	Wholesale, nondurable goods	100%		
% NAICS Group 79.0%	Retail Trade			
	21,745,670	100%		
	Industry Description		50-51	52-57, 59
441	Motor vehicle & parts dealers		10.4%	89.6%
442	Furniture & home furnishings stores		7.1%	92.9%
443	Electronics & appliance stores		7.1%	92.9%
444	Building material, garden equipment, & supplies dealers		29.3%	70.7%
445	Food & beverage stores			100%
446	Health & personal care stores		1.2%	98.8%
447	Gasoline stations			100%
448	Clothing & clothing accessories stores			100%
451	Sporting goods, hobby, book, & music stores			100%
452	General merchandise stores			100%
453	Miscellaneous store retailers		10.5%	89.5%
454	Nonstore retailers		5.1%	94.9%
7221-7224	Eating & Drinking Places			100%

SIC

SIC	SIC Group Employment / Industry Description	% NAICS Group	% in NAICS Classifications 4211-4221	441-8	451-4	7221-4
	27,668,088	99.2%	20.9%	34.6%	15.6%	28.0%
23.5%	Wholesale Trade	99.4%				
	6,509,333					
	Industry Description					
50	Wholesale trade - durable goods	100%	87.1%	12.6%		0.2%
51	Wholesale trade - nondurable goods	98.4%	91.5%	0.3%		3.7%
76.5%	Retail Trade	99.5%	20.0%	42.9%	36.6%	
	21,158,755					
	Industry Description					
52	Building materials, hardware, garden supply, and mobile home dealers	100%		95.1%	4.9%	
53	General merchandise stores	100%		0.0%	100%	
54	Food stores	98.4%		95.9%	0.2%	2.3%
55	Automotive dealers and gasoline service stations	100%		99.5%	0.5%	
56	Apparel and accessory stores	99.8%		99.8%		
57	Home furniture, furnishings, and equipment stores	97.4%		86.1%	11.3%	
58	Eating and drinking places					100%
59	Miscellaneous retail	99.2%		42.5%	56.3%	0.4%

Package

Unlike other industry groups, **Package** is defined by a broader set of industries. The data available for constructing comparable SIC and NAICS definitions required the inclusion of other products in paper, plastic, and glass manufacturing industries. However, the scope of the definition is the same, and the set of industries are inclusive of 99% of packaging industries' employment. In both the NAICS and SIC classification systems, "packaging" industries are not identified with a three-digit SIC or four-digit NAICS classification. There are three broad types of packaging for which a comparable set of SIC and NAICS industries were identified—paper, plastic, and glass. A fourth type, metal cans and containers, are excluded from the **Package** group, since it was not possible to identify a comparable set of industry classifications in the two systems within the limitations of the three-digit SIC and four-digit NAICS codes. In both the NAICS and SIC definitions, the set of industries included in **Package** refer to a broader set of industries, particularly in glass and plastic products manufacturing, in which packaging-specific industries are minor contributors to overall employment. Table A-8 (pp. 78-79) shows the comparable set of industries in the **Package** industry group.

In the NAICS, paper-based packaging industries account for 71% of employment in "Converted Paper Products Mfg" (NAICS 3222). In the SIC, paper-based packaging is identified with two three-digit industries—"Paperboard Containers and Boxes" (SIC 265) and "Miscellaneous Converted Paper Products" (SIC 267). While all of SIC 265 is considered to be packaging, only 49% of employment in SIC 267 is identified as specific to packaging industries. Moreover, only 74% of employment in SIC 267 is included in NAICS 3222, while the remainder (26%) is classified as belonging to "Plastics Product Mfg" (NAICS 3261). Together, the two SIC classifications account for 98% of NAICS 3222. With the exception of aluminum foil packaging, SIC 265 and 267 constitute the source industries for all of the paper-based packaging industries identified in NAICS 3222.

The NAICS definition of plastic products (NAICS 3261) includes 96% of SIC 308 and 26% of SIC 267. The source SIC classifications for all plastic-based packaging industries in NAICS 3261 come from SIC 267 and 308. Thus, the combination of plastic and paper product industries included in the definition of **Package** are inclusive of nearly all paper and plastic packaging industries. While glass containers are identified with SIC 322, the four-digit NAICS industry that includes glass containers also includes glass products industries identified with SIC 321, 322, and 323. With SIC 321 and 323 included, the SIC definition of glass products is the same as the NAICS, and glass containers constitute 16% of employment in both definitions. In both the NAICS and SIC definitions, the **Package** group is dominated by paper and plastic packaging. Although glass containers are of minor importance to glass products, the set of glass product industries is included in **Package** under the assumption that the printing-related activity in the industry is likely to be related to label-printing and design for glass containers. Glass products constitute only 10% of the total employment in the **Package** group. Plastic and paper industries constitute 90% of the industry group and 95% of the packaging-specific industry employment of **Package**.

Table A-8. NAICS and SIC Industries in Paper, Plastic, and Glass Packaging (Package)

NAICS Group Employment			SIC Group Employment					NAICS Industries		
Pkg Share of Group Total	Packaging Industries	All 4-digit Industries	SIC Group % of Total	Pkg Share of Group Total	Packaging Industries	All 3-digit Industries	% SIC in NAICS Group	3222	3261	3272
30%	398,132	1,333,292	99%	29%	388,198	1,344,728	98%	28%	61%	10%
	% NAICS Package — 66%	All Packaging — 393,165			% of SIC Package — 81%	All Packaging — 388,198				
	% NAICS Group — 28%	Paper Packaging — 264,570			% of SIC Group — 32%	Paper Packaging — 315,687				
		Paper Products (4-digit NAICS) — 377,839				Paper Products Industries (3-digit) — 426,720	100%	87%	13%	0%
Pkg Industries Share	NAICS code	Industry Description		Pkg Industries Share	SIC code	Industry Description				
71%	3222	Converted paper product mfg	98%	100%	265	Paperboard containers and boxes		100%		
	Packaging Industries detail - NAICS 3222			49%	267	Miscellaneous converted paper products		74%	26%	
	3222-1	Paperboard container mfg	100%		Packaging industries detail - SIC 267					
	3222-21	Coated & laminated packaging paper & plastics film mfg	100%		2671	Paper - coated & laminated, packaging		26%	74%	
	3222-23	Plastics, foil, & coated paper bag mfg	100%		2673	Bags - plastics, laminated, & coated		7%	93%	
	3222-24	Uncoated paper & multiwall bag mfg	100%		2674	Bags - uncoated paper and multiwall		100%		
	3222-25	Laminated aluminum foil mfg for flexible packaging uses	0%		2677	Envelopes		100%		
	3222-32	Envelope mfg	100%							

Table A-8. NAICS and SIC Industries in Paper, Plastic, and Glass Packaging (Package) (con't.)

NAICS Group Employment

Pkg Share of Group Total	Packaging Industries	All 4-digit Industries	SIC Group % of Total
		Plastic Packaging	
	% NAICS Package — 27%	107,411	
	% NAICS Group — 62%	Plastics Industries (4-digit) — 826,615	SIC Group Contribution
Pkg Industries Share	NAICS code	Industry Description	
13%	3261	Plastics product mfg	99%
	Packaging industries detail - NAICS 3261		
	3261-11	Unsupported plastics bag mfg	100%
	3261-12	Paper - coated & laminated, packaging (pt)	100%
	3261-3	Laminated plastics plate, sheet, & shape mfg	100%
	3261-6	Plastics bottle mfg	100%
		Glass Packaging	
	% NAICS Package — 5%	21,184	
	% NAICS Group — 10%	Glass Industries (4-digit) — 128,838	
Pkg Industries Share	NAICS code	Industry Description	
16%	3272	Glass & glass product mfg	100%
	Packaging industries detail - NAICS 3272		
	3272-13	Glass container mfg	100%

SIC Group Employment / NAICS Industries

Packaging Industries	All 3-digit Industries	% SIC in NAICS Group	3222	3261	3272
	Plastic Packaging				
% SIC Package — 13%	51,327				
% SIC Group — 59%	Plastic Industries (3-digit) — 789,170				
SIC code / Pkg Industries Share	Industry Description				
308 / 7%	Miscellaneous plastics products, n.e.c.	96%		96%	
Packaging industries detail - SIC 308					
3083	Laminated plastics plate and sheet			100%	
3085	Plastics bottles			100%	
	Glass Packaging				
% SIC Package — 5%	21,184				
% SIC Group — 10%	Glass & glass product mfg (3-digit SIC) — 128,838				
SIC code / Pkg Industries Share	Industry Description				
321-323 / 16%	Glass & glass product mfg	100%			100%
Packaging industries detail - SIC 322					
3221	Glass containers				100%

Apparel, Textiles, and Leather Goods

The **Apparel/Textiles** group consists of all industries that engage in the manufacture of textiles, apparel, and leather goods. None of the three-digit SIC industries is equivalent to a particular NAICS classification, even at a higher level of aggregation. As in the case of **W&R Trade**, NAICS classifications combine detailed classifications from different two-digit SIC industries into one NAICS industry. Thus, for example, NAICS 313 (Textile Mills) includes industries from "Apparel" (SIC 22) and "Textiles" (SIC 23), while "Apparel Manufacturing" (NAICS 315) includes both SIC-based "Apparel Industries" (SIC 231, 234-6, and 238) and "Textiles" (SIC 221-229). "Footwear and Leather Goods Mfg" (NAICS 3161-9) includes all of SIC 313 "Boot and Shoe Cut Stock and Findings", SIC 314 "Footwear, Except Rubber", and also adds SIC 302 "Rubber and Plastics Footwear", which is identified with rubber products in the SIC system. With the addition of SIC 302, the SIC and NAICS definitions of "Footwear and Leather Goods" are equivalent.

In total, the SIC-defined group accounted for 98.6% of all jobs in the NAICS-defined group in 1997. Most of the remainder is attributable to additions from a re-classification of some detail classifications in retail trade to apparel manufacturing. The 1997 data show that employment in the SIC classifications (identified in Table A-9) for the **Apparel/Textiles** group was 3% greater than that of the NAICS group. This difference reflects the NAICS re-assignment of 25.7% of the jobs from SIC 239 (at the four-digit level) to industries outside the **Apparel/Textiles** group. Of the re-assigned total (64,163 jobs), 53.4% were moved to **PRINT** (NAICS 323) and 46.6% to industries in the NAICS-defined **Other Mfg** group. Since the SOC data do not provide four-digit SIC information, it is not possible to separate the portion of SIC 239 that is excluded from the NAICS-based group. As a result, the SIC definition applied to the 2001 SOC data may overstate employment in core printing occupations in **Apparel/Textiles** while understating employment in the commercial printing specialization within the **PRINT** industry.

Table A-9. NAICS and SIC Industries in Apparel, Textiles, and Footwear & Leather Goods (Apparel/Textiles)

NAICS Code	% NAICS Group	NAICS Group Employment	SIC Group % of Total	% SIC Group	SIC	SIC Group Employment	% NAICS Group	% of Total in NAICS Classifications 3131-3, 3141-9	3151-9	3161-9
		1,434,175				1,477,761				
	43.9%	Textiles — 610,682	98.6%	38.0%		Textiles — 561,875	95.7%	48.6%	41.3%	5.7%
NAICS Code		Industry Description			SIC	Industry Description				
3131-3		Textile mills	96.8%		221-9	Textile mill products	99.3%	80.5%	18.8%	0%
3141-9		Textile product mills	97.2%							
	50.2%	Apparel — 718,423		56.1%		Apparel — 829,334				
NAICS Code		Industry Description			SIC	Industry Description				
3151-9		Apparel	99.9%		231-9	Apparel and other textile products	92.7%	19.1%	73.6%	0%
	5.9%	Footwear & Leather Goods — 84,493		5.9%		Footwear & Leather Goods — 86,552	100%			
NAICS Code		Industry Description			SIC	Industry Description				
3161-9		Leather & allied products	99.6%		311-319	Leather Goods	100%	0%	2.6%	97.4%
					302	Rubber and plastics footwear	100%			100%

NAICS Definitions of Publish and PRINT

In the SIC system, "Printing, Publishing, and Allied Industries" refers to SIC 27. This two-digit industry includes all the detailed classifications for both printing and print-based publishing industries. While the NAICS and SIC definitions of the printing and publishing industries are not exactly the same, the differences are small. Moreover, all employment in SIC 27 is included in the NAICS definitions. As Tables A-10 and A-11 show, the **PRINT** group (Table A-10) of industries is distinguishable from **Publish** (Table A-11) by a combination of three- and four-digit SIC classifications. In the NAICS, all the detailed classifications in **PRINT** are identified with the same four-digit classification, 3231 "Printing and Related Support Activities". All of the employment in the SIC classifications for printing are included in the NAICS definition. Moreover, as Table A-10 shows, employment in "Books and Magazine Printing", "Business Forms and Blankbooks", and "Support Activities for Printing" is the

Table A-10. NAICS and SIC Industries in Printing and Related Support (PRINT)

	NAICS Group Employment*	SIC Group % of Total		SIC Group Employment	% NAICS Group
	838,240	95.8%		803,171	100%
NAICS	Industry Description				
323100	Printing and Related Support Activities				
% NAICS Group	Commercial Printing		% SIC Group	Commercial Printing	
75.3%	630,861	94.4%	74.2%	595,792	
NAICS	Industry Description		**SIC**	Industry Description	
32311-3	Commercial (lithographic, gravure, flexographic)		275	Commercial Printing	
323114	Quick printing				
323115	Digital printing				
323119	Other commercial printing				
% NAICS Group	Books & Magazines		% SIC Group	Books & Magazines	
5.9%	49,104	100%	6.1%	49,104	
NAICS	Industry Description		**SIC**	Industry Description	
323117	Books		2732	Book printing	
% NAICS Group	Business Forms & Blankbooks		% SIC Group	Business Forms & Blankbooks	
8.9%	74,229	100%	9.2%	74,229	
NAICS	Industry Description		**SIC**	Industry Description	
323116	Manifold business forms		276	Manifold business forms	
323118	Blankbooks & looseleaf binders		2782	Blankbooks and looseleaf binders	
% NAICS Group	Support Activities for Printing		% SIC Group	Support Activities for Printing	
10.0%	84,046	100%	10.5%	84,046	
NAICS	Industry Description		**SIC**	Industry Description	
323121	Tradebinding & related work		2789	Bookbinding and related work	
323122	Prepress services		2791	Typesetting	
				2796	Plate making services	

* Of the 35,069 jobs added to commercial printing from other Source SIC industries, 98% reflect the re-classification of automotive and apparel trimmings in SIC 2396.

same in the NAICS and SIC definitions. While the NAICS definition of "Commercial Printing" includes additions from other source SICs (98% of which is attributable to SIC 2396), SIC 275 accounts for 94.4% of the total.

In publishing, the NAICS definition includes all but 836 jobs from the SIC classifications for the publishing industry. Employment in the newspapers and magazines sector of publishing are the same in both the NAICS and SIC definitions. "Book Publishing" and "Other Publishing" are the two categories where the NAICS and SIC definitions differ. The NAICS definition allocates a small fraction of "Book Publishing" to the "Other Publishing" category and includes additions from SIC 899 and SIC 733 to the "Other Publishing" category. Still, the SIC-defined publishing classifications account for 89.3% of employment in the NAICS classifications in the "Other Publishing" category.

While the **PRINT** industry consists of a single four-digit NAICS, the 2005 employment estimates for **Publish** include two four-digit NAICS classifications—NAICS 5111 "Newspaper, Periodical, Book, and Directory Publishers" and NAICS 5122 "Sound Recording Industries." The latter includes music publishers. The 1997 NAICS-SIC Census Tables indicate that music publishing employment accounts for 20.1% of all employment in this four-digit industry. In 1997, total employment in NAICS 5122 was 21,514 jobs, and there were only 4,335 employed in music publishing. In 2005, NAICS 5122 contributed less than 1% of employment in core printing occupations in **Publish** (a total of 380 jobs).

Table A-11. NAICS and SIC Industries in Print-Based Publishing (Publish)

		NAICS Group Employment	SIC Group % of Total			SIC Group Employment	% NAICS Group
		742,420	98.4%			731,128	99.9%
	NAICS	*Industry Description*			*SIC*	*Industry Description*	
	5111	Newspaper, periodical, book, and directory publishers					
% NAICS Group		*Publishing industries detail - NAICS 5111*		*% SIC Group*			
54.0%	51111	Newspapers	100%	54.8%	271	Newspapers	100%
18.6%	51112	Periodicals	100%	18.9%	272	Periodicals	100%
12.1%	51113	Books	100%	12.6%	2731	Books	100%
15.3%	Other publishing		89.3%	13.7%	Other publishing		
	51114	Database & directory publishing*			274	Other publishing NEC	100%
	51119	Other publishers			277	Greeting card publishers***	96.2%
	51223	Music publishers**					

*10,128 jobs in direct mail advertising services were assigned to NAICS 51114 from SIC 733. This constitutes 3.3% of SIC 733 (which has a total of 309,695 jobs). The remainder of SIC 733 (96.7%, or 299,567 jobs) is assigned to the Prof & Biz group.

**All of NAICS 5122 is assigned to publishing. Only the SIC-based publish industries are included in the SIC-defined group. SIC 899 is the other source SIC for music publishers. This is not assigned all to publishing because the 51223 share of SIC 899 total is 1.9%. SIC 899 also has 88.8% of its total assigned to the Prof & Biz group.

***836 jobs were excluded from Greeting Card Publish (SIC 277).

Estimating Print and Publish Shares of 'Books' for 2001

While the four-digit NAICS classifications clearly distinguish between printing and publishing industries, the two are not completely separable in the three-digit SIC classifications. For 2000 and 2001, employment data on occupations provided by the BLS was limited to three-digit SIC industry classifications. Since book printing and publishing constitute SIC 273, the BLS data did not separate the shares of employment that belong to Book Publishing (2731) from Book Printing (SIC 2732). Therefore, the **PRINT** and **Publish** shares of Books were estimated for 2001.

For the **PRINT** group, the SIC and NAICS definitions of book printing are equivalent. Table A-12 shows the employment in all occupations, production jobs, and non-production jobs in NAICS 3231 for 2000, 2001, and 2002, as reported in the 2002 Census. Employment in "Book Printing" (NAICS 323117) is also reported separately. With employment in book printing excluded, Table A-12 shows that book printing employment in all occupations was 6.6% of the total in all **other** classifications within the printing industry in 2000 and 2001. Similarly, book printing's share of production jobs' was the same for both years (7.4%). With respect to the rest of the **PRINT** industry, book printing's share of professional, administrative, and clerical occupational employment was 4.7%.

Table A-12. Employment in the Printing Industry, 2000, 2001 and 2002

Printing Industry Employment: Total, Production, and Non-Production		Census 2002		
		2000	2001	2002
Total Industry Employment				
323100	Printing and Related Support Activities	830,404	798,710	718,542
323117	Books	51,765	49,708	38,764
	Print Industry - Books	778,639	749,002	679,778
	Book Print Emp ÷ (Print Industry-Books)	6.6%	6.6%	5.7%
Employment in Production Jobs				
323100	Printing and Related Support Activities	597,687	573,919	515,019
323117	Books	41,418	39,584	30,764
	Print Industry - Books	556,269	534,335	484,255
	Book Print Emp÷(Print Industry-Books)	7.4%	7.4%	6.4%
Employment in Professional, Management, & Clerical Occupations (Non-Production Jobs)				
323100	Printing and Related Support Activities	232,717	224,791	203,523
323117	Books	10,347	10,124	8,000
	Print Industry - Books	222,370	214,667	195,523
	Book Print Emp÷(Print Industry-Books)	4.7%	4.7%	4.1%

With the exception of book printing, the BLS occupational employment data provided counts for each of the three-digit industries identified as belonging to NAICS 3231. As a consequence, occupational employment for printing (less books) is known, as is the combined total of book printing and publishing. The occupations of *Prepress Technician, Press Operator, Job Printer,* and *Bindery Worker* are classified by the BLS as "production." Book printing employment in these occupations was estimated in two steps. First, for each occupation, employment in Book Print was computed as 7.4%* Σ(SIC 275, 276, 278 & 279). As Table A-13 shows, this calculation of book printing employment was larger than the total in SIC 273 for the occupations of *Job Printer* and *Press Operator*.

For these occupations, all of the employment SIC 273 was allocated to book printing (SIC 2732). For the *Bindery Worker* and *Prepress Technician* occupations, the estimate was less than the total for SIC 273. The difference between the total (SIC 273 - estimate of SIC 2732) was allocated to Book Publishing (SIC 2731).

Table A-13. Employment Estimates of Prepress Technicians, Production Printers, and Bindery Workers for Book Printing and Publishing*

		Job Printer	Press Operator	Prepress Technician**	Bindery Worker
Printing Industry Total		**38,060**	**95,410**	**56,535**	**65,321**
SIC	*Industry Description*				
275-6, 278-9	Print - Books	36,600	89,760	52,640	60.820
275	Commercial Printing	33,460	79,080	42,500	46,470
276	Manifold Business Forms	1,800	7,090	2,190	2,780
278	Blankbooks, Looseleaf Binders, and Bookbinding	640	2,170	730	10,830
279	Service Industries For The Printing Trade	700	1,420	7,220	740
2732	Estimate of Book Print	1,460	5,650	3,895	4,501
	Calculated estimate	*2,708*	*6,642*	*3,895*	*4,501*
Publishing Industry Total		**7,080**	**21,080**	**19,715**	**8,539**
SIC	*Industry Description*				
271	Newspapers Publishing	5,090	14,390	12,400	1,710
272	Periodicals Publishing	1,010	2,850	2,780	3,450
274	Miscellaneous Publishing	790	1,610	1,800	1,150
277	Greeting Cards	190	2,230	1,700	40
2731	Book Publishing Estimate	0	0	1,035	2,189
273	*Book Print & Publish****	*1,460*	*5,650*	*4,930*	*6,690*

* Based on SIC 27 Production Occupational Employment, BLS 2001.

For SIC 27 (2-digit total), employment of Prepress Technicians was 76,250. Known employment in 3-digit industries (Print & Publish) totaled 74,550. In SIC 277, number of Prepress Technicians were suppressed (''). Estimate of number of Prepress Technicians employed in SIC 227 = SIC 27 employment - ∑3-digit industry employment.

***Procedure for Estimating Book Print & Publish Shares of SIC 273 Employment:
1) Calculate Book Print estimate based on Census, where production workers in Book Printing = 7.4%* ∑(SIC 275, 276, 278 & 279).
2a) If Book Printing Estimate ≥ SIC273, then SIC 2732 =SIC 273, and SIC 2731 =0.
2b) If Book Printing Estimate < SIC273, then SIC 2731 = SIC 273 - Estimate for SIC 2732

Table A-14 shows the same method applied to the occupations of *Graphic Designer* and *Desktop Publisher*. For these occupations, book printing's share was estimated with the percentage of non-production jobs reported in the Census. Hence, book printing employment was calculated as 4.7%* ∑(SIC 275, 276, 278 & 279). Note that, for both *Graphic Designers* and *Desktop Publishers*, the two-digit SIC 27 total was greater than the sum of the three-digit industries' totals. The difference was allocated in proportion to the **PRINT** and **Publish** shares of occupational employment based on three-digit counts.

Table A-14. Employment Estimates for Graphic Designers and Desktop Publishers in Book Printing and Publishing*

		Desktop Publisher	Graphic Designer
Printing Industry Total		**10,849**	**14,878**
SIC	*Industry Description*		
275-6, 278-9	Print - Books	10,350	14,210
275	Commercial Printing	6,030	11,480
276	Manifold Business Forms	680	390
278	Blankbooks, Looseleaf Binders, and Bookbinding	80	180
279	Service Industries For The Printing Trade	3,560	2,160
2732	Book Printing	486	668
	Share of 2-digit SIC 27 residual	*13*	*0*
Publish Industry Total		**14,941**	**19,012**
Industry Total (without residual share)		*14,924*	*--*
SIC	*Industry Description*		
271	Newspapers Publishing	6,010	10,880
272	Periodicals Publishing	3,040	3,800
274	Miscellaneous Publishing	2,740	2,870
277	Greeting Cards	0	110
2731	Book Publishing	3,134	1,352
	Share of 2-digit SIC 27 residual	*17*	*0*
273	Books	3,620	2,020
	Calculated estimate for SIC 2732	*486*	*668*
27	Printing, Publishing, and Allied Industries	25,790	33,880
	∑ 3-digit SIC employment	*25,760*	*--*

* Based on SIC 27 Production Occupational Employment, BLS 2001.

**Assign difference to industry in proportion to share of combined occupational employment total.

***Procedure for Estimating Book Print & Publish Shares of SIC 273 Employment.
1) Calculate Book Print estimate based on Census, where employment in non-production occupations = 4.7%* ∑(SIC 275, 276, 278 & 279).
2a) If Book Printing Estimate ≥ SIC273, then SIC 2732 =SIC 273, and SIC 2731 =0.
2b) If Book Printing Estimate < SIC273, then SIC 2731 = SIC 273 - Estimate for SIC 2732

Complex Industry Groups

There are several industry groups that span different industries. These groups combine industries with similar requirements for printing and are expected to have a similar configuration of employment for the various core printing occupations as a result. Industries identified with the same group (or cluster of industries within a group) share commonalities as to type of service, mix of private and public sector, and government regulatory constraints. **Educ & Health**, **FIRE**, and **Prof & Biz** Services constitute major industry groups with such complex industry compositions.

Education and Health

The list of comparable industry classifications in the **Educ & Health** group is divided into two tables. Table A-15 shows the overall importance of employment in the educational industries that are excluded from the Census, while Table A-16 (pp. 88-89) compares NAICS- and SIC-defined health service and health product industries. In Table A-15, industry shares for "Other Educational Services" were based on the 1997 Bridge Tables and applied to the 2001 BLS data on employment in NAICS 6114-5 and 6117.

Table A-15. NAICS and SIC Industries in Educational Institutions and 'Other Education Services' (Educ)

	NAICS Group Employment*		SIC Group % of Total		SIC Group Employment		% NAICS Group
	11,963,486		98.8%		11,815,080		100%
% NAICS Group	Educational Institutions (Public & Private)			**% SIC Group**	Educational Institutions (Public & Private)		
96%	11,464,210		100%	97%	11,464,210		
NAICS	*Industry Description*			**SIC**	*Industry Description*		
611100	Elementary and Secondary Schools			821	Elementary and Secondary Schools		
611200 & 611300	Junior Colleges, 4-year Colleges, Universities & Professional Schools			822	Colleges, Universities, Professional Schools, and Junior Colleges		
624300	Vocational Rehabilitation Services			833	Job Training and Vocational Rehabilitation		
% NAICS Group	Other Education Services**			**% SIC Group**	Other Education Services		
4%	499,276		70%	3%	350,870		
NAICS	*Industry Description*			**SIC**	*Industry Description*		
611400	Business Schools and Computer and Management Training			824	Vocational Schools		
611500	Technical and Trade Schools			829	Schools and Educational Services, n.e.c.		
611700	Educational Support Services						

* BLS industry data for 2001was used to compare SIC and NAICS industry shares of group employment. No census data on employment in public schools and colleges is available. Census does not report employment for NAICS 6111-3, SIC 821 and 822.

**The 2001 employment estimates for NAICS 6114-5 and 6117 were based on the 1997 Census Bridge Table, which shows that SIC 824 and 829 contributed 70% of the combined employment in these industries.

Table A-16. NAICS and SIC Industries in Health Services and Products (Health)

% NAICS Group	NAICS Group Employment	SIC Group % of Total	% SIC Group	SIC Group Employment	% NAICS Group
	12,804,235	99.1%		12,711,572	99.8%
% NAICS Group	Offices & Clinics of Health Care Providers	SIC Group % of Total	% SIC Group	Offices & Clinics of Health Care Providers	% NAICS Group
26%	3,313,287	97%	25%	3,202,343	99.99%
NAICS	Industry Description		SIC	Industry Description	
6211	Offices of physicians	100%	801	Offices and clinics of doctors of medicine	
6212	Offices of dentists	100%	802	Offices and clinics of dentists	
6213	Offices of other health practitioners	100%	803	Offices and clinics of doctors of osteopathy	
6214	Outpatient care centers	100%	804	Offices and clinics of other health practitioners	
6219	Other ambulatory health care services	36%	809	Miscellaneous health and allied services, n.e.c.	
% NAICS Group	Hospitals	SIC Group % of Total	% SIC Group	Hospitals	% NAICS Group
39%	4,933,038	100%	39%	4,933,038	100%
NAICS	Industry Description		SIC	Industry Description	
622	Hospitals		806	Hospitals	
% NAICS Group	Nursing & Residential Care Facilities	SIC Group % of Total	% SIC Group	Nursing & Residential Care Facilities	% NAICS Group
19%	2,470,723	100%	19%	2,470,723	100%
NAICS	Industry Description		SIC	Industry Description	
6231	Nursing care facilities		805	Nursing and personal care facilities	
6232	Residential mental retardation/health & substance abuse facility		836	Residential Treatment Service	
6233	Community care facilities for the elderly				
6239	Other residential care facilities				
% NAICS Group	Home Health Care Services	SIC Group % of Total	% SIC Group	Home Health Care Services	% NAICS Group
7%	948,989	100%	7%	948,989	100%
NAICS	Industry Description		SIC	Industry Description	
6216	Home health care services		808	Home health care services	

Table A-16. NAICS and SIC industries in Health Services and Products (Health) (con't.)

% NAICS Group	Medicines, Laboratory Equipment & Supplies (4-digit industries)	SIC Group % of Total	% Med-Specific
9%	1,138,198	99.6%	
	Medical- Specific Share		
	758,244	99.5%	65.5%

NAICS	Industry Description	SIC Group % of Total	% Med-Specific
3254	Pharmaceutical & medicine mfg	100%	100%
6215	Medical & diagnostic laboratories	100%	0%
3391	Medical equipment & supplies mfg	99%	23%
3345	Navigational, measuring, medical, & control instruments mfg	99.6%	100%
	Medical-Specific Classifications		100%
334510	Electromedical & electrotherapeutic apparatus mfg		0%
334516	Analytical laboratory instrument mfg		100%

% SIC Group	Medicines, Laboratory Equipment & Supplies (3-digit SIC industries)	% NAICS Group
9%	1,156,479	96.4%
	Medical- Specific Share	
	757,013	99.7%

SIC	Industry Description	% NAICS Group	Contribution to NAICS Classifications			
			3254	3391	3345	6215
283	Drugs	100%	100%			
381	Search and navigation equipment	100%			100%	
382	Laboratory apparatus	92.0%		7%	85%	
384	Surgical, medical & dental instruments & supplies	92.7%		68%	24%	
385	Ophthalmic goods	100%		100%		
387	Watches, clocks, watchcases, and parts	100%		100%		
807	Medical and dental laboratories	100%		21%		79%

While Table A-16 shows Census employment in 1997 and Table A-15 relies on 2001 BLS estimates, the two subgroups appear to be nearly equivalent in terms of overall employment. Overall, the combined employment in the NAICS-defined **Educ & Health** group is slightly larger, having 1% more jobs than are included in the SIC definitions. All employment in SIC classifications for Education is included in the NAICS definition. For the Health Sector, 23,509 jobs were assigned to non-Health NAICS classifications. All but 282 of these jobs reflect re-assignments to other industries within the manufacturing sector.

The educational industries included in the Census are limited to SIC 824 and 829 and NAICS 6114-5 and 6117. These industries comprise the category "Other Educational Services" in Table A-15. While all of SIC 824 and 829 were included, these two industries account for only 70% of the NAICS sub-group employment in educational support services. The additions to NAICS are attributable to the re-classification of four- and five-digit SIC classifications that represent a small fraction of their three-digit industry. For example, 66% of employment in NAICS 6117 (Educational Support Services) comes from SIC 8748, "Educational Testing and Evaluation Services" (a total of 19,472 jobs). The 1997 employment in the three-digit SIC 874 (Management and Public Relations Services) totaled 948,109, and 94% of these jobs were assigned to NAICS classifications identified with the **Prof & Biz** group. Since the detail SIC classifications for decomposing employment in SIC 874 were unavailable, the total was classified as belonging to the SIC-defined **Prof & Biz** group. In most cases, when a three-digit SIC is divided among industries identified with different groups, all of the SIC industry is assigned to the group that has the most employment. In all, the NAICS educational services industries include 148,406 jobs from non-education industries. In total, these additions account for approximately 1% of the overall employment in the NAICS definition of the Education sector. Moreover, since all of the exclusions are confined to "Other Educational Services", the SIC and NAICS definitions are equivalent for the cluster of industries in "Educational Institutions". The latter cluster accounts for 96% of all employment in NAICS educational service industries and 97% of the SIC-defined Education subgroup.

As Table A-16 shows, the industries in the Health sector are divided into five clusters of related industries. Three of these clusters—"Hospitals", "Nursing & Residential Care Facilities", and "Home Health Care Services"— are completely comparable. Moreover, six of the NAICS classifications in "Offices & Clinics of Health Care Providers" (NAICS 6211-14) are comprised solely of the SIC industries in the same category. Most of the difference between NAICS and SIC definitions of "Health Care Services" has to do with the miscellaneous NAICS classification 6219 (Other Ambulatory Health Care Services). Only 13% of the employment in SIC 809 (Miscellaneous Health and Allied Services, n.e.c.) is assigned to NAICS 6219. Instead, 87% of SIC 809 is identified with NAICS 6214 (Outpatient Care Centers) and employment from SIC 809 accounts for 81% of NAICS 6214. The majority (64%) of NAICS 6219's employment comes from transportation services related to local ambulance and rescue services (55% of SIC 4119) and air ambulance or MedEvac services (12% of SIC 4522). The shares of the SIC three-digit industry for these medically-related classifications were small, and were therefore excluded from the SIC definition of "Health Services". The excluded contributions from SIC 4119 and 4522 account for 96% of the employment differences between the NAICS and SIC "Health Services and Products" definitions.

Of the industries in "Medicines, Laboratory Equipment & Supplies", only medicines are directly comparable (SIC 283 and 3254). To construct a comparable group of industries inclusive of medical laboratory equipment and supplies, it was necessary to include two industries that had no sub-specializations related to that category (SIC 381: Search and Navigation Equipment, and SIC 387: Watches, Clocks, Watchcases, and Parts). The SIC classifications that are identified specifically with medical equipment and supplies are divided among three NAICS classifications: 6215 (Medical and Diagnostic Laboratories), 3391 (Medical Equipment and Supplies Manufacturing), and 3345 (Navigational, Measuring, Medical, and Control Instruments).

Excluding drugs, medical-specific employment in the other SIC health-products' classifications totaled 572,004. SIC 384 (Surgical, Medical and Dental Instruments and Supplies) was responsible for 49% of these jobs. Specializations within SIC 384 resulted in 68.2% of employment assigned to NAICS 3391, 24.5% to NAICS 3345, and 7.3% distributed among other NAICS manufacturing industries. To construct a comparable group of SIC and NAICS industries that included most of the employment in the SIC specializations (SIC 8072, 384, 385, and 23% of SIC 382), it was necessary to identify those three-digit SICs that were major contributors to NAICS 3354. By including SIC 381 and 387 (100% assigned to NAICS 3354) along with SIC 382 and 384, the group of SIC industries in this category accounted for 484,794 of the 486,815 jobs in NAICS 3354 (99.6%), and 294,094 of the 297,019 jobs in NAICS 3391 (99.0%). The SIC group is larger because all of SIC 384 and 382 are included, whereas the combined employment in NAICS 3345 and 3391 accounts for only 92.7% of SIC 384 and 92.0% of SIC 382. Note that NAICS 3345 and 3391 included employment from other three-digit SICS, which accounted for 2,021 and 2,925 jobs, respectively.

Finance, Insurance, and Real Estate

In the **FIRE** group, "Finance" includes both public and private banking institutions, securities and other investment industries. "Insurance" includes both insurance carriers and brokers. As Table A-17 shows, all of the employment in the SIC-defined industries in finance and insurance industries are included in the NAICS definition of the two industry clusters. In "Real Estate", only 92% of employment within the SIC definition was included in the NAICS cluster. Still, total employment in the SIC-defined **FIRE** group represents 99% of the total employment in the NAICS definition. There is no difference between the NAICS and SIC definitions of "Insurance". All of the employment differences reflect differences in the definitions of banking/credit and real estate. Exclusions from the SIC definition of "Real Estate" account for 61.7% of all SIC-excluded employment in NAICS **FIRE**. All other exclusions reflect differences between the SIC and the NAICS definitions of "Other Financial Investment Vehicles" (NAICS 525).

With respect to "Finance", only NAICS 5222 and 5223 include additional employment from non-finance SIC industries. Two four-digit SIC classifications contributed 46,105 additional jobs. From SIC 7389, 23,642 jobs were re-classified from "Credit Card Processing Industries." SIC 7389's contribution represents 4.2% of employment in NAICS 5222. From "Pawn Shops," a retail trade industry in the SIC (part of SIC 5932), 22,436 jobs were included in the NAICS definition of "Activities Related to Credit Intermediation" (NAICS 5223).

Table A-17. NAICS and SIC Industries in Finance, Insurance, and Real Estate (FIRE)

% NAICS Group	NAICS Group Employment	SIC Group % of Total		% SIC Group	SIC Group Employment	% NAICS Group
	6,952,463	99%			7,042,525	98.1%
% NAICS Group	Finance	98%		% SIC Group	Finance	% NAICS Group
51%	3,533,700			49%	3,479,708	100%
NAICS	Industry Description			**SIC**	Industry Description	
5211	Monetary authorities - central bank	100%		60	Depository institutions	
5221	Depository credit intermediation	100%		61	Nondepository credit institutions	
5222	Nondepository credit intermediation	96%		62	Security and commodity brokers, dealers, exchanges, and services	
5223	Activities related to credit intermediation	86%		679	Miscellaneous investing	
5231	Securities & commodity contracts intermediation & brokerage	100%				
5232	Securities & commodity exchanges	100%				
5239	Other financial investment activities	97%				
5259	Other investment pools & funds	100%				
5331	Patent owners & lessors	100%				
% NAICS Group	Insurance			% SIC Group	Insurance	
33%	2,327,306	100%		33%	2,327,306	100%
NAICS	Industry Description			**SIC**	Industry Description	
5241	Insurance carriers			63	Insurance carriers	
5242	Agencies, brokerages, & other insurance related activities			64	Insurance agents, brokers, and services	
% NAICS Group	Real Estate			% SIC Group	Real Estate	
16%	1,117,249	98.3%		17%	1,194,083	92%
NAICS	Industry Description			**SIC**	Industry Description	
5311	Lessors of real estate	96%		651	Real estate operators (except developers) and lessors	98%
5312	Offices of real estate agents & brokers	100%		653	Real estate agents and managers	88%
5313	Activities related to real estate	100%				

PRINTING OCCUPATIONAL EMPLOYMENT, HIGH-WAGE JOBS, & INDUSTRY SOURCES OF GROWTH – 2001 TO 2005

Employment in "Educational, Religious, and Charitable Trusts" (SIC 6732) accounts for 81% of SIC 673. All of SIC 6732 was assigned to "Grantmaking Foundations" (NAICS 8132), while only 7,887 jobs from SIC 673 were included in "Other Financial Investment Activities" (NAICS 5239). Since most of the employment (68%) of NAICS 8132 comes from SIC 839 ("Social Services, n.e.c."), NAICS 8132 is not considered to be a "Finance" industry, and SIC 673 was also excluded from the SIC-definition of finance. Hence, the included SIC-defined finance industries account for only 96.8% of employment in NAICS 5239.

In the SIC definition, the real estate industries consist of "Real Estate Operators (Except Developers)"(SIC 651) and "Real Estate Agents and Managers" (SIC 653). The comparable NAICS classification for these industries is the three-digit NAICS classification code 531. Within the NAICS definition of "Real Estate", employment from SIC 651 and 653 accounts for 98.3% of the total. Excluded from the NAICS definition was employment related to "Stadium and Arena Owners" (part of SIC 6512). From SIC 6531, jobs related to "Cemetery Management" and "Condominium or Coop Owner Associations Engaged in Property Management" were also excluded. In total, SIC 6531 accounted for 91.1% of the real estate-related employment excluded from the NAICS definition. NAICS 531 includes 18,673 jobs from an SIC source in transportation services (SIC 4225: Lessors of Mini-Warehouses and Self Storage Units). Even so, the SIC-defined real estate industries accounted for 98.3% of the employment in NAICS 531.

Professional and Business Services

The industries in the **Prof & Biz** group consist of four comparable clusters—**Advertise**, **Biz Support & Design**, **Computer Services**, and **Other Prof**—and one category, **Mgmt/HQ**, that is not comparable. Table A-18 (pp. 95-96) compares the NAICS and SIC definitions of the four comparable clusters. (Note that **Mgmt/HQ** is excluded from this table. The NAICS definition of **Mgmt/HQ** is identified with one four-digit classification, "Management of Companies and Enterprises" (NAICS 5511). "Offices of Holding Companies" (SIC 671) is the only source SIC unique to NAICS 5511. "Corporate Subsidiary & Regional Management Offices" account for 95.2% of NAICS 5511. These offices are treated as "auxiliaries" in the SIC system, and are not included in any three-digit SIC industry totals. Hence, for 2001, employment in SIC 671 constitutes the sole source for estimating employment in the **Mgmt/HQ** category.)

In total, 97.8% of the employment in the SIC-definition of **Prof & Biz** (without **Mgmt/HQ**) is included in the NAICS definition of the group. The NAICS definition excludes some of the employment in five three-digit SIC industries (733, 737, 738, 874, and 899) that are wholly counted in the SIC-defined group. Most of the employment in SIC 733, 737, 738, 874, and 899 is in the NAICS definition. However, 295,699 of the 4,398,556 jobs in the combined total employment of these industries were excluded from the NAICS classifications. Taken together, the exclusions account for 6.7% of the jobs in these five three-digit SICs. The greatest number of excluded jobs in the NAICS definition is identified with "Miscellaneous Business Services" (SIC 738), accounting for 47.3% of the total (139,866 jobs) from all five SIC classifications.

Of greater importance is the combination of three-digit industries that define the NAICS industry clusters. The SIC-defined **Advertise** consists of one three-digit SIC (731). While the SIC classifications included in the **Prof**

&Biz group account for 92.9% of the NAICS classification for the advertising industry (NAICS 5418), only 60.3% of the NAICS definition comes from SIC 731. The SIC definition of **Biz Support & Design** contributed 32.6% of the jobs in NAICS 5418. This re-allocation accounts for only 1.8% of employment in the SIC-defined cluster. The industries in "Mailing, Reproduction, Commercial Art and Photography, and Stenographic Services" (SIC 733) are the source for 63% of the employment from the SIC-defined **Biz Support & Design** cluster that was re-classified and included in the NAICS definition of **Advertise**. The clusters that are most alike in the NAICS and SIC definitions are **Other Prof** and **Computer Services**. All employment in the SICs that define **Other Prof** is included in the NAICS definition of this industry cluster. Moreover, 98.4% of the contributions to the NAICS definition of **Other Prof** from the SIC-defined **Prof & Biz** group are attributable to the SIC definition of **Other Prof**. In the SIC definition, **Computer Services** consists of all the employment in SIC 737 and SIC 899. The NAICS definition of **Computer Services** includes only 17.1% of employment in SIC 899, with 71.7% of this SIC identified with the NAICS definition of **Biz Support & Design**. However, 45.2% of employment in "Internet Publishing and Broadcasting" (NAICS 5161) is attributed to SIC 899. Moreover, this SIC is the only industry identified in the **Prof & Biz** group that was a known contributor to NAICS 5161. For these reasons, all of the employment in SIC 899 was included in the SIC definition of **Computer Services** for constructing a comparable industry in 2001. With the exception of NAICS 5161, all other computer service specializations identified by the NAICS are derived totally from SIC 737 (Computer Services). Excluding the contribution of SIC 899 to the NAICS-defined **Biz Support & Design** cluster, the industries included in the SIC definition of this cluster contributed 97.5% of all jobs in the NAICS definition. Thus, three of the four clusters are nearly the same in the SIC and NAICS definitions. Only **Advertise** is significantly different.

In 2001, 57.8% of *Press Operators* and 56.8% of *Prepress Technicians* in the **Prof & Biz** group were employed in SIC 733. While the NAICS definition of **Advertise** included 27.7% of employment in SIC 733, 63.1% of this SIC's employment is identified with **Biz Support & Design**. Therefore, some of the employment gains in *Press Operators* that are attributed to **Advertise** should be attributed to the re-definition of SIC 733 instead. Most of the employment gains are likely to reflect changes in **Advertise** itself. Considering the magnitude of the reductions in employment identified with **Biz Support & Design**, it is unlikely that a substantial share of these losses would be the result of a minor change in the definition of these services associated with NAICS definition of **Advertise**.

Table A-18. Comparable Industry Clusters in the Professional and Business Services Industry group (Prof & Biz)*

					Industry Clusters in Professional & Business Services*							
					Advertise	Biz Support & Design		Computer Services			Other Professional	
					5418	5414 & 5416	5611-14, 5617-19	5112 & 5415	5161	5181-2, 5191	5411-13	5417 & 5419
Whole group					3.1%	5%	53%	8.2%	0.1%	2.8%	22%	3.6%

NAICS side

	NAICS Group Employment	SIC Group % of Total		SIC Group Employment	% NAICS Group
	12,768,756	96.1%		12,567,259	97.6%

Advertise — % NAICS Group 3.3%

% NAICS Group	NAICS	Industry Description	NAICS Group Employment	SIC Group % of Total		SIC	Industry Description	SIC Group Employment	% SIC Group	% NAICS Group
3.3%	5418	Advertising & Related Services	417,214	92.9%	Advertise	731	Advertising	251,580	2%	100%

Advertise cluster: 100%

Business Support & Design — % NAICS Group 57.9% | % SIC Group 60.7%

	NAICS Group Employment	SIC Group % of Total		SIC Group Employment	% NAICS Group
	7,390,441	98.5%	Business Support & Design	7,628,705	95.5%

NAICS	Industry Description	SIC Group % of Total	SIC	Industry Description	% NAICS Group	Advertise 5418	5414 & 5416	5611-14, 5617-19	5112 & 5415	5161	5181-2, 5191	5411-13	5417 & 5419
5416	Mgmt. Scientific & technical consulting	99.7%	874	Mgmt. & public relations services	94%	4.1%	41.0%	48.9%					
5414	Specialized design services	99.9%	733	Mailing, Reproduction, Commercial Art and Photography, and Stenographic Services	96.7%	27.7%	19.9%	43.3%					5.9%
5611	Office Administrative Services	100%											
5612	Facilities Support services	100%	732	Consumer Credit Reporting Agencies, Mercantile	100%			100%					
5613	Employment services	100%	734	Services To Dwellings and Other Buildings	100%			100%					
5614	Business Support services	98.0%	736	Employment services	100%		1.3%	98.7%					
5616	Investigative & security Services	97.9%	738	Miscellaneous business services	91.3%	0.7%	3.2%	83.8%			0.6%	1.8%	1.3%
5617	Services to buildings & dwellings	92.5%											
5619	Other Support services	100%											

*With the exception of the Mgmt/HQ cluster.

Table A-18. Comparable Industry Clusters in the Professional and Business Services Industry group (Prof & Biz)* (con't.)

Industry Clusters in Professional & Business Services*

	Advertise	Biz Support & Design		Computer Services			Other Professional	
NAICS	5418	5414 & 5416	5611-14, 5617-19	5112 & 5415	5161	5181-2, 5191	5411-13	5417 & 5419
5112				72.6%		22.0%		
5161		71.7%			11.1%	6.0%		
5191						100%		
5411							100%	
5413							100%	
5412							100%	
5417							17%	83%

Main cluster detail

% NAICS Group / NAICS	Industry Description (NAICS)	SIC Group % of Total	% SIC Group	SIC	Industry Description (SIC)	% NAICS Group
	Computer & Related Information Services — 1,406,051	99.0%	12.3%		Computer Services — 1,545,470	90.1%
11%						
5112	Software Publishers	100%		737	Computer services	94.5%
5415	Computer Systems Design and Related Services	100%				
5161	Internet Publishing and Broadcasting	45.2%		899	Other services, nec	88.8%
5181	Internet service providers & web search portals	100%				
5182	Data processing, hosting, & related services	100%				
5191	Other information services	100%		823	Libraries & archives	100%
	Other Prof — 3,555,050	90.3%	25%		Other Prof — 3,141,504	100%
27.8%						
5411	Legal services	100%		654	Title Abstract Offices	100%
				811	Legal Services	
5413	Architectural, engineering, & related services	100%		871	Engineering, architectural, & surveying services	100%
5412	Accounting, tax return prep, bookkeeping, & payroll services	71.4%		872	Accounting, auditing & bookkeeping	100%
5417	Scientific research & development services	100%		873	R&D & testing services (excluding non-commercial research orgs)	100%
5419	Other professional, scientific, & technical services	69.2%				

*With the exception of the Mgmt/HQ cluster.

ABOUT THE PRINTING INDUSTRY CENTER AT RIT

The Printing Industry Center at RIT is dedicated to the study of major business environment influences in the printing industry precipitated by new technologies and societal changes. The Center addresses the concerns of the printing industry through research initiatives and educational outreach. The Center creates a forum for printing companies and associations worldwide to access a neutral platform for the dissemination of knowledge that can be trusted by the industry, to share ideas, and to build the partnerships needed to sustain growth and profitability in a rapidly changing market.

The research agenda of the Printing Industry Center at RIT and the publication of research findings are supported by the following organizations:

Printing Industry Center
Rochester Institute of Technology
College of Imaging Arts and Sciences
55 Lomb Memorial Drive
Rochester, NY 14623
http://print.rit.edu